KING of the OILERS

The Story of the U.S.S. Chiwawa AO-68

To Rhonda:
See you on the dance floor.
Best Wishes,
Jon L. Strupp
12-7-07

JON L. STRUPP

ISBN 13: 978-1-59298-191-5
ISBN 10: 1-59298-191-7
Library of Congress Catalog Number: 2007930182

Book design and typesetting: Mighty Media, Inc.
Printed in the United States of America

First Printing: July 2007
11   10   09   08   07   5   4   3   2   1

Beaver's Pond Press, Inc.

7104 Ohms Lane, Suite 216
Edina, Minnesota 55439 USA
(952) 829-8818
www.BeaversPondPress.com

To order, visit www.BookHouseFulfillment.com or call 1-800-901-3480. Reseller and special sales discounts available.

Front cover: USS *Chiwawa*, U.S. Navy photo taken March 8, 1944. Crewmen's signatures from the 1944 Thanksgiving menu.

Dedicated to the men and families of
The King of the Oilers: USS *Chiwawa* AO-68.

In memory of
James O. Strupp WT1c
USS *Chiwawa*, May 15, 1943–December 13, 1945
July 11, 1922–December 2, 2003

Table of Contents

⚓

Foreword

⚓

THERE ARE MANY WHO LOOK FORWARD TO THE COMPLETION OF
this book chronicling the events, activities, and personnel of the USS
Chiwawa. Jon Strupp, son of James Strupp, Watertender 1c, aboard
the *Chiwawa*, has invested many hours and not a few dollars in researching life aboard this ship during her service in the Atlantic and
Pacific theaters during World War II.

Without setting out to do so, Jon has uncovered much evidence
of personal interest to the shipmates and their families. Many crew
members and their families await news of fellow crewmen, justly
proud of the part they played. While spending the better part of
three years of their lives on the *Chiwawa* a sense of "family" developed among guys facing danger together many of the days they
served. Most remember with pride that the *Chiwawa* was known
as *"King of the Oilers"* for the speed and efficiency displayed in the
main responsibility of refueling ships at sea, as well as the many
varied tasks required of oilers in the successful waging of war in
two oceans. Without fuel, which such unglamorous vessels brought

to other ships and planes, the war would have lasted much longer at a much higher cost of men and material.

These men were lawyers, doctors, teachers, college students, engineers, and just plain American workers. Husbands, fathers, boyfriends, and strangers unfamiliar to the ways of military service came from many different locations. Many had never been at sea or even smelled the unique scent of salty ocean air. But they were all fashioned into a functioning, efficient bunch – proud of their ship and grateful to be serving with men who might one day have a part in saving their lives.

May the telling of the events that helped shape the lives of these men of such varied backgrounds bring back memories to the men of the *Chiwawa* and to the families and friends of those who have passed on to their place of peaceful rest.

Thanks, Jon, for what you have done and will do. As the popular song says, Thanks for the memories!

Lt. j.g. Leslie V. Ottman USNR (Retired)
Navigator, USS *Chiwawa* AO-68
February 2002

Introduction

⚓

My dad was 44 years old when I was born. I knew little about his early adulthood, and he never talked much about his Navy days. I got things in bits and pieces – an experience here or a funny story there. He also passed down to me some pictures and souvenirs. Several of my relatives and some of Dad's friends served in the military during World War II. Stories of their experiences awakened in me an interest in that period of history.

My dad and I grew up in profoundly different circumstances. I went to college, lived at home, and worked. For my dad and his generation, early-adult-life was far more complex. By the age of 22 he had seen four continents and was living every day as if it were his last. I now understand why he became upset with me when he felt I wasn't living up to my potential. I always wanted to know more about his Navy experiences, so I set out to do some research. At first, it was slow going (this was before the days of the Internet). I couldn't find out much about the USS *Chiwawa*, the ship he served aboard. The ship, a Navy oil tanker, wasn't even mentioned in *Jane's Fighting Ships of World War II*. When people think of the Navy, they picture battleships, destroyers, cruisers, and aircraft carriers – not oil tankers. But without the tankers other ships couldn't go anywhere.

One of the goals of this book is to give recognition to the often-overlooked men of the oiler fleet for enduring dangerous missions and making an important contribution to the war effort. It's my way of saying "thank you" for their service to our country. With the use of U.S. Navy records, eyewitness accounts, and memorabilia as my guide, I have chronicled the proud history of the USS *Chiwawa* AO-68. I hope to make this record as accurate as possible to dispel accumulated rumors and scuttlebutt. My only regret in this project is that the Internet didn't come along sooner so that I could have located more surviving members of the crew. I have met a lot of great people while researching the *Chiwawa,* and I want to thank every one for their priceless contributions.

Chapter I

Development of the Oiler Fleet

⚓

"Our ships sailed on water, but they moved on oil, and the demand never ceased."

Rear Adm. W. R. Carter USN
Beans, Bullets and Black Oil

"It is the function of the Navy to carry the war to the enemy so that it will not be fought on U.S. soil."

Fleet Admiral Chester W. Nimitz USN

THE PROCESS OF REFUELING AT SEA WAS DEVELOPED DURING the beginning of the twentieth century. Ships turned from coal to oil as fuel to feed their hungry boilers for propulsion. As the demand for a ship's range increased, a system of support vessels and replenishment procedures were required. The oilers were born. In U.S. Navy definitions all tankers are termed Auxiliary Oilers (AO), but unofficially, the term "oiler" is reserved for tankers that can refuel other ships at sea. Ships not equipped to refuel at sea and only carried bulk oil from port to port are referred to as "tankers."

The first oilers were built shortly before World War I. A promising young lieutenant from the submarine force, Chester W. Nimitz, was assigned to USS *Maumee* AO-2 as chief engineer and executive officer. He was instrumental in developing equipment and procedures for refueling at sea as the convoy system was used for the first time to transport supplies and troops from the U.S. to Europe during World War I. He was promoted to lieutenant commander before leaving the *Maumee* and returning to the submarine force.

With the end of World War I, Japan took control of Germany's possessions in the Central Pacific (the Marshall Islands, the Caroline Islands, and the Marianas Islands, except Guam) and was seen as a major threat to the United States. During the interwar years it was realized that a plan would have to be developed to defend U.S. possessions and interests over the immense distances of the Pacific. The Joint Army-Navy Board, developing Plan Orange for a possible war with Japan, realized that the logistical feat of taking a war as far as the Philippines was going to take the development of a fast fleet of ships and auxiliaries to support them. By the mid 1930s war clouds began to gather again. Replenishment-at-sea techniques were refined and improved, but the aging ships were coming to the end of their useful lives.

In order to keep Plan Orange viable, the Navy saw a need for new oilers. President Franklin D. Roosevelt signed into law the Merchant Marine Act of 1936, calling for the development and maintenance of a strong merchant marine capable of serving as a naval and military auxiliary in time of war or national emergency. The act paved the way for construction of a new oiler fleet under the New Deal Recovery Act's provision for public works.

On January 3, 1938 an agreement was signed between the Maritime Commission and Standard Oil of New Jersey for the construction of the first twelve National Defense Tankers. These tankers were built for commercial use, but construction provisions enabled the ready conversion of the ships for military use. With that in mind, the men who eventually became the *Chiwawa* crew – like their ship – were not primarily intended for warfare. The men came from cities and towns all over the United States. They were factory workers, farmers, coal miners, salesmen, clerks, students, and teachers.

Duty would call both man and machine together to defend their country.

Chapter 2
Enter the Mighty Chiwawa

⚓

WITH THE ATTACK ON PEARL HARBOR PLUNGING THE UNITED
States into war, the Navy implemented its plan to convert commercial tankers into military vessels. The Navy also purchased civilian tankers already under construction. With the pressing need for ships, the Navy accepted several military tanker designs.

Bethlehem Steel Company at Sparrows Point, Maryland, built the ship that would eventually bear the Chiwawa name. This ship, the ss *Samoset*, was commissioned for Socony-Vacuum (Mobil) Oil Co. *Samoset* was launched June 25, 1942, as U.S. hull #251505 sponsored by Mrs. H. G. Smith. The name was changed on September 16, 1942, to USS *Chiwawa* AO-68 (pronounced she-wa-wa, although many pronounced it che-wa-wa, like the little dog). It was named after a river in Washington State that flows through the Wenatchee National Forest. All oilers were named after rivers with Native American names until the end of World War II. Work was halted on her until November 1, when the Navy bought her. Then came the alterations necessary for readying her as a U.S. Navy vessel. On December 24, 1942, the ship was commissioned USS *Chiwawa* AO-68. The *Chiwawa* was designated a T3-S-A1 design: "T" stood for tanker, "3" meant longer than 500 feet, "s" stood for single screw propeller, and "A1" meant first design of its kind.

The *Chiwawa*'s dimensions were: displacement of 5,782 tons (21,077 tons fully loaded), length 501 feet 8 inches, beam 68 feet, and draft 30 feet 8 inches.

The ship could haul up to 134,000 barrels of oil (a barrel equals 42 gallons). Its top speed was 15 knots, and its armaments included a 5-inch gun, four 3-inch guns, four-twin 40mm guns, and four 20mm guns.

The Navy sought to obtain as many *Chiwawa*-class ships as possible because of their superior speed. Bethlehem Steel had orders to build 15 *Chiwawa*-class ships, but delivered only five due to building-capacity constraints. Those five ships include the AO-68, USS *Enoree* AO-69, USS *Escalante* AO-70, USS *Neshanic* AO-71, and USS *Niobrara* AO-72.

A crew of 188 enlisted men and 25 officers gathered on the cargo deck at 2 P.M. for commissioning ceremonies on December 24, 1942. The SS *Samoset* was commissioned USS *Chiwawa* AO-68 by order of the 5th Naval District and command was given to Cmdr. Harold F. Fultz USN, the *Chiwawa*'s first captain. The chaplain said a prayer asking for God's protection over the ship and her crew. The captain read his orders. The commission pennant was hoisted, followed by the national ensign. The chief boswain mate piped, "Set the watch," and the USS *Chiwawa* was in full commission. Roland Durant, S1c, and Don Demers, Cox, said the crew was greeted with a Christmas dinner of coffee, half-cooked potatoes, and Spam sandwiches – the enlisted mess hall was not yet fully operational. The officers' mess hall was apparently in better shape, as the captain commented during his commissioning speech about the fine dinner they had just been served. Edmund Corriera, GM1c, brought a small Christmas tree aboard ship, decorated it with toilet paper from the ship's supply, and placed it at one of the gun stations.

On December 30 the *Chiwawa* received its first load of Navy Special Fuel Oil totaling 137,928 gallons from Esso barge #2. During the following two months, shipyard workers continued to put finishing touches on the *Chiwawa*'s construction. During the "shakedown" period, which is a test cruise under operating conditions looking for possible faults or defects and to familiarize the crew with a new ship, the crew cruised the Chesapeake Bay where rough seas were encountered and the ship was tossed about like a cork. Almost all of the green crew became seasick. In Navy-speak, they were "green" or inexperienced seafarers. Water ballast was added to help steady the ship. The first refueling exercise was done on January 17, 1943, with an unnamed light cruiser.

That first crew was a mix of sailors. Chief Boswain Mate James Spence had 13 years of Navy experience serving on many different ships before he was stationed aboard the *Chiwawa*. He was like a father figure to many of the new sailors, some of whom were away from home and smelling salt air for the first time in their lives. Other seasoned sailors – like Harry Baynes, Cox, who had experience on another oiler (uss *Kaweah* ao-15) – did their part to acclimate the new recruits to life and work at sea.

Refueling at sea is a precise and delicate operation. Ships had to leave the convoy to refuel, preferably bearing into the wind and maintaining a constant heading, speed, and distance between the oiler and ship to be refueled once connected. The oil lines could snap if the two ships strayed apart, spraying oil everywhere and making the deck a slippery mess. The ships also risked collision if they veered too close during refueling. It was sometimes necessary to refuel two ships at once, compounding the potential for danger. In addition to refueling the fleet, the *Chiwawa* also fulfilled a role as a training ship for new sailors who would later transfer their expertise to other vessels.

Don Demers, Cox, realized the dangers of serving on an oiler. He told his mother he was serving on a destroyer so she wouldn't worry so much. He recalled those first days on the *Chiwawa* as a mess boy in the Chief Ward Room. From 6 a.m. to 6 p.m. he made coffee, prepared meals, and cleared the tables. Unfortunately, he knew nothing about drinking coffee, much less making it. The men had to tell him that the coffee grounds had to be changed every day.

For the *Chiwawa*'s first cruise into hostile waters, she left her home port of Norfolk, Virginia, on February 13, 1943, bound for Aruba. The *Chiwawa* and uss *Mattaponi* ao-41 were escorted by World War I-era destroyers uss *Decatur* dd-341, uss *Dickerson* dd-157 and uss *Upshur* dd-144. The *Chiwawa* refueled the destroyers on February 16. The ships arrived in Aruba on February 18 and the *Chiwawa* received 126,882 gallons of Navy Special Fuel Oil. On February 20 the *Chiwawa* left Aruba with USS *Mattaponi* bound for New York escorted by USS *Stansbury* DD-180. During the trip the ships encountered a storm on the evening of February 24. The *Chiwawa* deck log reported injuries to three of the crew. Edward Cocot, S1C, gave more details of the incident. He said barrels of oil were tied to the handrail on the well deck. A wave of green seawater broke over the deck, knocking three barrels loose. Three men were sent to secure the barrels. The pitching and rolling of the ship made the task more difficult as one of the barrels fell on the men. Orman T. Buckley, BM2C, suffered a left frontal area compound skull fracture, multiple contusions, and abrasions of both legs. Dominic S. Dygon, S2C, suffered a compound fracture of his lower left leg, and Horton B. Phillips, S1C, bruised his ankle and foot. The *Chiwawa* arrived in New York on February 25 without further incident.

By December 1942, 1,965 Allied ships had been lost to U-boats. To thwart the U-boat menace, a convoy system was developed in which ships traveled in large groups. A similar system was deployed during World War I. Oilers fueled the destroyers and destroyer escorts that defended the convoy, which traveled in a zigzag pattern to keep the U-boats guessing at the route and final destination. The Allies had developed technology such as radar to combat the U-boats, but the subs still posed an ominous threat.

The *Chiwawa*'s first convoy was UGS-6: "UGS" stood for U.S. Gibralter slow eastbound convoys of Operation Torch, which supplied the campaign in Africa. Convoy Commodore, Cmdr. John W. W. Cumming USN (Ret.), boarded the *Chiwawa* on March 3 and was stationed there during the convoy. The convoy of 45 ships, plus seven destroyers armed with the latest centrimetric-wavelength radar, left New York at 6 P.M. on March 4, 1943, bound for Casablanca. The Germans had deciphered an intelligence slip in a message to the U.S. Coast Guard off of the coast of Greenland. The message revealed the course of the slow-moving convoy. On March 7, the Norwegian motor ship *Tamesis*, sailing independently from Lobito Bay to New York with general cargo, encountered the convoy. The *Tamesis* captain changed course to avoid the convoy, but the convoy commodore signaled instructions for him to change to a westerly course, and though he felt this was against all common sense, he found he had to follow orders and collided with SS *Alcoa Guard*. The *Tamesis* sank in a few minutes two hundred miles northeast of Bermuda. Due to faulty radio communication, only one ship, SS *Richard A. Alvey* knew of the collision. It dropped out of the convoy to pick up 76 survivors – 57 from M/S *Tamesis* and 19 from SS *Alcoa Guard*. Fifty of the SS *Alcoa Guard* crew remained on board. The SS *Richard A. Alvey* escorted the SS *Alcoa Guard* to Bermuda.

A group of 17 German submarines set out to meet the convoy east of the Azores, picking dusk as the most advantageous time of attack because eastbound convoys could be silhouetted against the setting sun. The subs traveled in three "wolf packs" named by German U-boat Control in Berlin: Unverzaget (Intrepid), Wohlgemut (Optimistic), and Tummler (Dolphin). U-130, an imminent threat with 24 kills already to its credit, on March 10 made its first sighting of the convoy and shadowed it. Allied radar discovered U-130 ahead of the convoy on March 12. The destroyer USS *Champlin* DD-601 was sent to investigate and spotted U-130 on the surface. The destroyer fired its 5-inch forward gun, attempted to ram her, and finally sunk the U-boat with depth charges after the sub executed a crash dive to evade the onslaught. All 53 hands on board the U-boat were lost.

The first victim of the wolf pack in the convoy was SS *Keystone*. Slowed by boiler trouble, she fell 50 miles behind the convoy and was steaming alone as none of the escorts could be spared. The ship didn't take the route designated for stragglers, but followed the convoy and was torpedoed by U-172 on March 13 about 450 miles west of the Azores. One torpedo struck on the port side of the #5 hatch. The explosion blew a hole in the hull between #5 hold and the poop deck, destroyed the steering engine and steering gear, buckled the deck, disabled the 4-inch stern gun, and flooded the shaft alley. Five minutes after the hit a fire started and one of the aircraft carried on deck caught fire. The initial explosion killed one armed guard sailor and a merchant seaman. They were the only casualties suffered by the ship, which was abandoned. The Portuguese ship *Sines* rescued the remaining 71 survivors.

On March 14, the convoy received some redemption when USS *Rhind* DD-404 picked up 22 survivors in a lifeboat from the Norwegian merchant ship *Thorstrand* that had been sunk on March 6 by U-172. The ship departed Liverpool, England, on February 27 bound for

St. John, New Brunswick, traveling alone with 1,500 tons of general cargo.

At 6:53 P.M. on March 15 SS *Wyoming* was hit by two torpedoes from U-524 and sank in eight minutes. The U-boat penetrated the escort screen and fired torpedoes from a mere 600 yards. USS *Champlin* picked up 127 survivors. On March 16, USS *Wainwright* DD-419 discovered U-515 on the surface and fired on the U-boat, forcing it to crash dive. A well-laid pattern of depth charges followed, damaging the diesel engines and making the hydrophone system inoperable on U-515.

At 6:56 P.M. on March 16 SS *Benjamin Harrison*, hit by a single torpedo from U-172, was crippled beyond repair. Many ships in the convoy began firing in many directions. The *Chiwawa* fired one shot from its 5-inch gun at an object near station 64. It ceased fire due to proximity to other ships. Great confusion arose aboard the SS *Benjamin Harrison*. Some men shouted to abandon ship before the ship's master gave the order, and men began leaving the ship in a chaotic manner. The torpedo explosion had damaged one of the lifeboats and in their haste two more were improperly launched, causing the occupants to fall into the sea. USS *Rowan* DD-405 rescued three survivors and SS *Alan A. Dale* rescued the remaining 65. USS *Rowan* scuttled the ship by gunfire about 150 miles east north east of Terceira, Azores. Two officers and one armed guard died in the sinking. At sunrise on March 17, U-158 fired into the convoy and missed. At sunset, U-167 fired a salvo of four torpedoes at random into the convoy, two of which passed beneath the *Chiwawa*. One of the torpedoes that missed the *Chiwawa* hit SS *Molly Pitcher* about 500 miles west of Lisbon, Portugal, inflicting serious damage. USS *Champlin*, USS *Rowan*, and SS *William Johnson* picked up 2, 18, and 46 survivors, respectively. U-521 finished off the crippled freighter later the same day. Two of the 24-man armed guard and two merchant seamen perished in the sinking. Many more attacks were likely thwarted by radar-equipped escort ships that trolled for a "scent" of the wolf packs when the seas were calm and drove them off. On March 18, Liberator aircraft dispatched from Port Lyautey, Morocco, arrived and also assisted in driving away the U-boats. The U-boats broke off contact on March 19. The convoy arrived in Casablanca on March 21 without further incident. The four ships the Germans totaled 28,018 tons. The *Chiwawa* crew earned a battle star for their European African Middle Eastern Campaign Ribbon for the perilous encounter with the enemy.

Robert Shook, SM2C, took star sights on the *Chiwawa* flying bridge with CQM Frank Ward during convoy UGS-6. Shook said the *Chiwawa* was the lead ship in the middle column when suddenly they heard the explosion of a torpedoed ship in the rear of the column. The ship was hit foremast and split in half. Frank had a stopwatch in his pocket and timed the sinking in seven-and-a-half minutes. Warren H. Ray, MM2C, was in *Chiwawa*'s fire room. He said they heard explosions and wanted to go topside to investigate. CMM Theodore Shippie (a retired chief called back to duty during WW II) growled at them to go back to their posts. "You'll leave when I tell you to," he said. Donald Demers, an ammunition loader on the *Chiwawa*'s 5-inch gun, remembered seeing a light bobbing in the distance after one of the ships was attacked. Some crew members called the gunnery officer a "90-day wonder," an officer who usually had a college degree or some college training and graduated from an accelerated Navy training program in 90 days as a commissioned officer.

French cargo ship SS *Wyoming* sinks after being torpedoed by U-524 on March 15, 1943. Photo taken by William D. Gustin from USS *Champlin* DD-601. (Used with permission.)

The gunnery officer instructed the gun's crew to train the gun on the light. Then he hollered the order to fire, hiding behind the gun's splinter shield as he told them the light was the conning tower of a submarine. Demers recalled, "I believe the gun captain told him it was actually a lifeboat. The gunnery officer overrode him: That's a submarine, damn it. I said, 'Fire.'" A single shot was fired. Demers added, "That ship had five men missing, and they were all in that life raft." Edmund Corriera said one of the officers jumped into the captain's motor launch and shouted, "Give me some food and water!" After they got back to the states, Cmdr. Fultz said, "My enlisted men performed very well, I only wish I could say the same for the officers." Demers said the gunnery officer who gave the order to fire was not aboard the next time the ship left port.

The author obtained a copy of the convoy report written by Convoy Commodore, Cmdr. John W. W. Cumming. Average speed of the convoy was 8.73 knots. On March 11, the *Chiwawa* refueled destroyers USS *Wainwright* DD-419, USS *Trippe* DD-403, USS *Mayrant* DD-402, USS *Rowan* DD-405, USS *Rhind* DD-404, and USS *Champlin* DD-601 escorting the convoy. In the morning of March 12, the remaining destroyer, USS *Hobby* DD-610, was refueled. The ships SS *Wyoming*, SS *Molly Pitcher*, and SS *Benjamin Harrison* were all in the middle column when they were torpedoed. The Commodore suggested that armed guard officers and as many of their men as practicable should, before going to sea, visit a sub base in the States or be permitted to see a sub underway in its various stages of visibility, from wholly on the surface to only periscope visible. That, he said, would be valuable because the convoy engaged in dangerous panic firing after the torpedoing of SS *Benjamin Harrison*. The following morning the Commodore issued the following message: "It is assumed everyone thought and did his best last night. Fire control is important, but so is self-control. Had there been subs in all the directions of firing last night there would be no convoy today. Destroy the enemy but don't let us succumb to panic and destroy each other. I hope there were no casualties. Keep alert at all times." No casualties whatsoever from gunfire were reported to the Commodore.

Sunset quickly became a dreaded time of day for the *Chiwawa* crew since that was when the U-boats were most likely to attack. The crew adopted the song "St. Louis Blues" by W.C. Handy as its unofficial theme song. As the sun went down the song took on a new meaning. Part of the lyrics are:

> I hate to see that evening sun go down
> I hate to see that evening sun go down
> Since the woman I love
> She has left this town
> If I'm feeling tomorrow like I feel today
> If I'm feeling tomorrow like I feel today
> I'll pack my bags and make my getaway

Chapter 3
Delivering the Goods

⚓

AFTER THEIR 'BAPTISM OF FIRE,' THE *Chiwawa*'s CREW MEMBERS remained in Casablanca, acted as a station tanker, refueled nine destroyers and unloaded two P-38 fighter planes originally loaded onto the cargo deck on March 2 in New York.

Casablanca was not quite the exotic and romantic destination depicted by Hollywood. An old Arab section of town, Old Medina, was exceptionally dangerous because Americans were not well-liked there, members of the crew said. It offered open-air markets selling everything from fresh meat from a kiosk to vendors walking around selling water from a goatskin. Sailors were required to stay in groups and not wander about aimlessly. Orders were issued for visits to Old Medina. The crew received rules with a map denoting a specific route to follow, and the duration of the visit was limited. If the group didn't return on time, then the shore patrol was sent in to find them. The shore patrol was staffed by Navy personnel, usually volunteers, who acted as police while a ship was in port. Many interviews with *Chiwawa* veterans recalled robberies, stabbings, and other close calls.

Mischief did abound, too. Don Demers, Cox, recalled that a trained monkey belonging to a boy in Casablanca was secreted aboard the ship. An officer, after discovering the monkey business, ordered the new "crew member" back to shore.

Many items were bartered or sold to the locals, too. Many of the crew looked "fat" leaving the ship, as they smuggled their mattress covers under their uniforms to be sold for $5 apiece to women who welcomed the material to make dresses. The locals also craved cigarettes, Parker 51 pens, candy, and combs.

Instructions for the officer in charge of personnel touring the Old Medina section of Casablanca.

The *Chiwawa* received 34,550 gallons of diesel oil from an oil barge. The ship participated in Convoy GUS-6 departing Casablanca on April 11 and arriving in Norfolk, Virginia, on April 28 at 9:37 P.M. The convoy consisted of 44 merchant ships, escorted by seven

American destroyers, three French destroyers, two minesweepers, a tugboat, an attack cargo ship, and two oilers. On April 17, the *Chiwawa* refueled the French destroyer *Tempête* along with USS *Simpson* DD-201, USS *Broome* DD-210, and USS *Rhind* DD-404. On April 22 the *Chiwawa* refueled USS *Simpson*, USS *Broome*, and all three French destroyers. On April 17 personnel on the *Tempête* were seen taking pictures of the *Chiwawa*. U.S. officers requested the commanding officer of the *Tempête* to destroy the film. During the convoy destroyers detected U-boats and dropped depth charges, though no engagements were reported. The crew was aware of the ever-present danger and kept its battle skills sharp with frequent drills while going about the business of delivering the goods. Convoy Commodore, Cmdr. John W.W. Cumming, had high praise for the *Chiwawa* in his convoy report commending the work of commanding officer Cmdr. Harold F. Fultz and the communications group (coding section and visual signal force). Cumming also noted how the *Chiwawa*'s commander maneuvered and handled the ship in an excellent manner from and to station as convoy guide while offering his cooperation. Cmdr. John W. W. Cumming completed his duties as convoy commodore and left the *Chiwawa* on April 29.

Also on April 29, the *Chiwawa* discharged its cargo of Navy Special Fuel Oil and diesel oil. After the cargo was discharged the ship moved to the Naval Operating Base in Norfolk, where the USS *Alcor* AR-10 moored along side the ship and began various repairs.

On May 4, the *Chiwawa* departed Norfolk with USS *Chemung* AO-30 and USS *Howard* DMS-7 as escort. The ships arrived in Aruba on May 9. Aruba was known for its tropical climate and "magic carpet rides." Houses of prostitution were off-limits to Navy personnel, and violators had to answer to the shore patrol. So prostitutes would roam the streets with a small carpet rolled under their arm, asking sailors if they would like a ride on the "magic carpet." Willing customers would hail a taxi to drive out to the beach, where the couple could conduct their business.

The *Chiwawa* loaded Navy Special Fuel Oil and gasoline and departed with the same two ships on May 10. The ships arrived in Norfolk on May 15 and the *Chiwawa* delivered gasoline to a gasoline barge. On May 16 the *Chiwawa* loaded diesel oil. The *Chiwawa* left Norfolk on May 18 with USS *Osprey* AM-56 as escort. Encountering fog during the trip, the ships arrive in Argentia, Newfoundland, on May 21. The *Chiwawa* refueled an unnamed aircraft carrier with 36,666 gallons of 100 octane gasoline on May 21. On May 24, the *Chiwawa* and *Osprey* departed Argentia bound for Norfolk. The ships arrived on May 27 and the *Chiwawa* reported to the Navy Yard for an overhaul.

There was always a constant flow of men to and from the *Chiwawa*. On May 28, 1943, 21 of Pennsylvania's sons reported for duty. They were recruited mostly from the Pittsburgh and surrounding area and went to boot camp at Great Lakes, Illinois. They were Joseph Kestler, Arthur Krieg, Bruner Lange, Gordon Lawson, Stanley Lesick, Larry Lingenfelter, William Liptak, Charles Fox, John Freker, Charles Gartland, William Hall, Murray Hoover, Edward Harkey, Paul Harvison, Ray Kern, Richard Catlin, Russell Chatfield, Bruce Churchfield, Joseph Curcio, Frank Dufour, and Francis Dugan.

On June 6 the overhaul was complete. The ship received radar, a diesel fire pump, and two 40mm guns. On June 8 the *Chiwawa* departed Norfolk with USS *Enoree* AO-69 and SS *Sabine Sun* and escorted by minesweepers USS *Osprey* AM-56 and USS *Auk* AM-57. On June 9 USS *Enoree* notified the other ships that they had a man overboard. The *Chiwawa* executed a series of 45-degree turns to search for the man while USS *Osprey* stood back to attempt a rescue. An airplane in the area was also notified of the incident. After searching for 45 minutes the man was not recovered, the search was discontinued, and the ships continued their voyage. On June 12 the *Chiwawa* made emergency 45-degree turns and USS *Osprey* dropped depth charges due to a sound contact. The ships arrived in Port Arthur, Texas on June 13. The *Chiwawa* loaded diesel oil, gasoline, and Navy Special Fuel Oil on June 13 and 14. The same ships departed Port Arthur on June 15 and arrived in Norfolk on June 20. The *Chiwawa* unloaded its cargo and loaded 200 drums of kerosene and 500 drums of gasoline. On June 23 the *Chiwawa* departed with USS *Merak* AF-21 escorted by USS *Palmer* DM-5 bound for Bermuda. The ships arrived in St. George, Bermuda, on June 24 and the *Chiwawa* delivered its cargo. On June 28 the *Chiwawa* participated in a refueling-at-sea exercise with USS *Palmer* and eight destroyer escorts. On June 29 the *Chiwawa* departed Bermuda with USS *Merak* and USS *Palmer* bound for Norfolk, arriving on July 1. The *Chiwawa* reported to the

Navy Yard for modification of the 40mm gun mounts for cartridge case removal. Repairs were made to the bow, stern, and boilers, and other minor work was done. The work was completed on July 8, and the crew members loaded Navy Special Fuel Oil.

On July 8, Cmdr. H. F. Fultz was detached from the *Chiwawa*, and on July 11 his executive officer, Lt. Cmdr. John P. Goza, assumed command of the ship. On July 6, 17-year-old Seaman 2c Guy Ken "Tex" Wood (after the war he changed his name to Ken Wood) reported for duty aboard the *Chiwawa* at Norfolk, Virginia. The *Chiwawa* departed Norfolk on July 12 with USS *Ringgold* DD-550 as escort and arrived in New York on July 13. On July 17, the day after his 18th birthday, Tex met Myrna Lois Nelson, a nursing student at Methodist Hospital in New York. They started dating, and Tex arranged for other *Chiwawa* sailors to date Myrna's friends. Tex announced on their second date, "I'm going to marry you." Myrna's response was, "Sailor, you can dry next week's wash on that line." They did get married and had 52 wonderful years together until Ken's death in 1996.

Ken and Myrna Wood in 1944.

The Allies began the invasion of Sicily – Operation "Husky" – on July 10, 1943. The liberation of the Italian mainland began on September 9 with Operation "Avalanche" at Salerno. The buildup for the invasion of France had also begun even though it was not planned until the spring of 1944. The *Chiwawa*'s role shifted to support the demand for men and supplies on these new fronts.

On July 14, seven army trucks were loaded aboard the *Chiwawa*'s cargo deck. The *Chiwawa* left New York for another crossing of the Atlantic on July 17 with convoy AT-54A. The convoy consisted of six U.S. Army transport ships carrying soldiers escorted by a cruiser, eight destroyers, and one escort aircraft carrier. On July 21 the *Chi-*

wawa refueled seven destroyers, and on July 24 refueled five destroyers. The convoy arrived in Greenock, Scotland, on July 26 without incident, although they encountered heavy fog on July 21 and 22. Scotland quickly became a favorite destination for the crew. Its landscape was beautiful and its people were very friendly to the Yanks. The mayor of Greenock declared the crew guests of honor of the city, and the locals welcomed the crew into their homes for food and drink, Jim Strupp, WT1c, recalled. Michael Campise, MM2c, said he remembered singers greeting them. There were also parties and dances held for the men in local pubs, said Harry Baynes, Cox.

On July 27 a floating crane and cargo vessels came along side the *Chiwawa* and unloaded the army trucks from the cargo deck. The *Chiwawa* also transferred Navy Special Fuel Oil to the British Royal Fuel Auxiliary ship *Thermol* and made more deliveries on July 28 and 29. On July 30 the *Chiwawa* delivered Navy Special Fuel Oil to RFA *Julianna*. On August 1 the *Chiwawa* refueled USS *Hilary P. Jones* DD-427 and USS *Doyle* DD-494 with Navy Special Fuel Oil and pumped more Navy Special Fuel Oil to RFA *Thermol*.

The *Chiwawa* participated in convoy TA-54A leaving Greenock, Scotland, on August 2. The convoy consisted of six U.S. cargo and transport ships, eight destroyers, one cruiser, and one escort aircraft carrier. Heavy fog was encountered on August 6 and 7. On August 7 the *Chiwawa* refueled eight destroyers. While refueling the USS *Doyle* DD-494, the tow line parted and the destroyer veered sharply to port, thus parting the forward and aft hoses. The refueling was aborted. On August 11 the *Chiwawa* left the convoy with USAT *Sea Train Texas*, USS *Greene* DD-266, and USS *Dickerson* DD-157. The group headed for Norfolk, Virginia, arriving on August 12. The *Chiwawa* discharged its cargo of Navy Special Fuel Oil and diesel oil to the dock. On August 15 the *Chiwawa* reported to the Norfolk Navy Yard for various projects throughout the ship.

The *Chiwawa*'s home port of Norfolk, Virginia, was a sleepy little town before the war that found itself saturated with military personnel almost overnight. Friction erupted between locals and visitors. Norfolk quickly became known as "Shit City" to military personnel, as signs in some residents' yards read, "Dogs and Sailors stay off the grass."

Shortly after reporting for duty to the *Chiwawa* on August 12, 1943, Lawrence T. Richardson Sr., CM2c, received a letter from his wife, Hazel, announcing the birth of their first son, Lawrence Jr., on August 23. "A fine boy weighing 7 pounds, 7 ounces," she wrote.

On September 1 the *Chiwawa* departed the Norfolk Navy Yard and joined USS *Salamomie* AO-26 and USS *Mattapponi* AO-41, escorted by USS *Nuthatch* AM-60 and USS *Osprey* AM-56 to form Task Unit 29.3.4. The task unit arrived in New York on September 2. The *Chiwawa* was loaded with gasoline and bunker fuel oil. On September 5, 1943, the *Chiwawa* was underway in Convoy UT-2 from New York to the United Kingdom stopping at the ports of Swansea, Wales, and Milford Haven. The convoy consisted of six U.S. cargo and transport ships, six oilers (including the *Chiwawa*), one tanker, six British transport ships, one battleship, and 14 destroyers. Evidence of the constant danger of German U-boats is recorded in the September 5 diary entry of Minneapolis native LaVerne Rogers, S2c, who was 18 years old at the time: "The tin cans (destroyers) have already dropped three ash cans (depth charges) when we were only three hours out of New York." Mike Campise, MM2c, remembered that the depth charges exploded so close to the *Chiwawa* that screws from the floor plates popped up.

LaVerne Rogers, S2c.

Arriving in Swansea on September 15 to deliver gasoline, the crew witnessed the massive destruction of the Blitz for the first time. James Veacock, Ptr2c, remembered that six blocks around the refinery were leveled. Rogers reported in his diary on September 18, "Swansea had a population of about 165,000 and several sections of the town were bombed out, with two or three square blocks wiped out completely. In another part of town the houses were leveled flat. Children beg for chewing gum, pennies and cigarettes by asking, 'Got some gum, chum?'" On September 19 the ship traveled about 40 miles to Milford Haven and anchored out about three miles from land.

On September 20 the *Chiwawa* started its return to Norfolk in Convoy TU-2. The convoy consisted of four U.S. Army transport ships, six oilers (including the *Chiwawa*), two tankers, and one Dutch transport ship escorted by one battleship, twelve destroyers, and one destroyer escort. LaVerne Rogers heard three large depth charge explosions on September 21 that sounded very close. The rest of the trip passed without incident, and the ship arrived in Norfolk on September 30.

On October 4 Navy Yard workmen arrived to make a routine overhaul to the ship. The work was completed on October 17. On October 21 diesel engines, parts, and 25 MK-6 depth charges were loaded aboard the cargo deck. An inspection crew from USS *Mattaponi* AO-41 boarded the *Chiwawa* on October 23 to test the crew's battle-readiness. The drill was used to examine the crew's skill in all phases of defending the ship, including submarine and air attack, damage control, executive control of the ship in case the captain was killed, and abandoning the ship. The *Chiwawa* left Norfolk on October 25 with Convoy UGS-22. The convoy consisted of 64 ships escorted by five destroyers, six destroyer escorts, and an air support group of one escort aircraft carrier and three destroyers.

Rogers said in his October 27 diary entry that he is studying history, math, typing, and English in his spare time and that he plans on studying as much as he can because he knows it will help him later in life. He added, "If I don't watch out I'll come out of the Navy with a college education."

On October 28 the *Chiwawa* refueled one destroyer escort and delivered fuel and fresh provisions to another destroyer escort. Rogers' October 28 diary reported an alert given to the convoy the night before that a sub was in the area. The guns were manned for about an hour and the convoy detoured. Sub alerts followed almost every night thereafter out of concern that a sub was on their trail. On October 29 the *Chiwawa* refueled 2 sub chasers and on October 30 refueled a destroyer. On October 31 Rogers wrote that two ships in the convoy collided the night before, with one ship taking on water so fast that its pumps were kept running at all times. They couldn't get a report on the other ship's condition, but bet it's having trouble too.

On November 1 Rogers wrote that, "We broke two 10-inch lines and had to cut another one, and the cans that we were refueling broke three hoses. Altogether they wrecked about $5,000 worth of equipment." The *Chiwawa*'s war diary gave more details of the incidents. While refueling USS *Hobby* DD-610, the after fuel hose parted due its deteriorated condition. USS *Kalk* DD-611 veered starboard while refueling and broke the forward fueling hose. USS *Evarts* DE-5 veered to port and then sharply to starboard and broke the tow line and spring line. The forward hose line was cut loose before it parted. Two other destroyers were refueled without incident.

On November 2 one sub chaser was refueled and the refueling of another was aborted due to heavy seas and darkness. Another fuel hose was lost due to heavy sea on November 3 while refueling a sub chaser. On November 4 the *Chiwawa* refueled six destroyers. On November 5 and 6 fresh provisions were transferred to sub chasers. On November 7, Rogers noted that a gunner's mate shot himself through the hand. On November 8, two destroyers were refueled by the *Chiwawa*. Nine destroyers and 2 sub chasers were refueled by the *Chiwawa* on November 9

The *Chiwawa* arrived in Casablanca on November 10. Rogers wrote on November 11, "We didn't have very much to do during the last few days but the important thing is that we landed in Casablanca Wednesday afternoon at 1730 (5:30 P.M.). We passed a few French ships that were sunk in the harbor, lying on their sides: the battleship Jean Barte and two French destroyers. The town is very modern in its buildings but not in its people. The buildings here would amaze you. They are the latest thing in modern architecture. You can see soldiers of every country here but the majority of them are French. Of the French there are about five kinds. Foreign Legion and the regular French army (Free French), and the rest are made up of French Colonials. The American Red Cross has its station here and the only thing they offer free is prophylactics. It may seem nice to you folks at home to be able to visit the different countries but to the mere sailor it's just a bunch of hooey. I suppose it is because we see only the bad side of everything. If you could see some of the dirty ragged urchins that roam the streets you would wonder how any parent could let her child go out like that. It was almost as bad as England was. The kids in England were begging for everything but when you told them to scram they went. Over here they can't understand you so they just keep on begging."

While in Casablanca the crew was kept busy pumping diesel oil, kerosene, and Navy Special Fuel Oil to destroyers, patrol craft, a yard oiler, a French tanker, and a Naval Operating Base barge. The diesel engines, parts, and 25 MK-6 depth charges were removed from the cargo deck and replaced with three landing barges for transport to Norfolk.

The *Chiwawa* started its return voyage to Norfolk from Casablanca at 11:30 P.M. on November 18 in Convoy GUS-21. The convoy consisted of 51 ships plus five destroyers and six destroyer escorts, along with an air support group of one escort aircraft carrier and three destroyers. The air support group left the convoy November 22. Rogers' November 22 diary entry states, "This is the fourth day out and haven't had any excitement as yet. We lost a kid while we were refueling the other day. He was handling lines on the bow of his destroyer and a wave came and toppled him overboard. We could see him as he floated past and the look on his face was one I wouldn't care to see again. They sent a can back to look for him and it threw a line to him but he was so weak that he let go and sank. That makes the fourth guy we have lost on all the trips that I've been on. This kid fell off the first can that we fueled yesterday and after the accident we quit for the day." On November 22 and 23 three destroyers were refueled each day by the *Chiwawa*. Six destroyer escorts were refueled by the *Chiwawa* and fresh provisions were also delivered to one of the destroyer escorts on November 24. The *Chiwawa* refueled three destroyers on November 27.

The crew celebrated Thanksgiving on November 25 while en route back to the states from Casablanca in Convoy GUS-21. The November 30, 1943, edition of *The Oil Spout*, the ship's newspaper, reported, "A magnificent meal was served to the men with all the trimmings of a traditional Thanksgiving meal. Tommy Moore worked for days dreaming up the ideas. Alexander 'Cookey' Cook, ex-yeoman, present ship's butcher thought of the menu and saw it through to completion. Tony Cappella and Big Joe Charbonneau gave those birds the tenderest of care with every cook and baker taking their off watch time to lend a hand to see serving go off smoothly. The menu below was put together by Wallace Schillem and the office

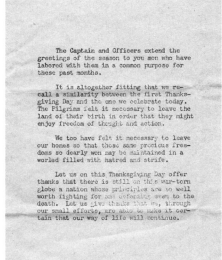

The Captain and Officers extend the greetings of the season to you men who have labored with them in a common purpose for these past months.

It is altogether fitting that we recall a similarity between the first Thanksgiving Day and the one we celebrate today. The Pilgrims felt it necessary to leave the land of their birth in order that they might enjoy freedom of thought and action.

We too have felt it necessary to leave our homes so that those same precious freedoms so dearly won may be maintained in a worled filled with hatred and strife.

Let us on this Thanksgiving Day offer thanks that there is still on this war-torn globe a nation whose principles are so well worth fighting for and defending even to the death. Let us give thanks that we, through our small efforts, are able to make it certain that our way of life will continue.

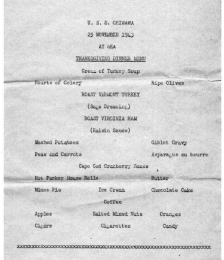

U. S. S. CHIWAWA
25 NOVEMBER 1943
AT SEA
THANKSGIVING DINNER MENU

Cream of Turkey Soup

Hearts of Celery   Ripe Olives

ROAST VERMONT TURKEY
(Sage Dressing)

ROAST VIRGINIA HAM
(Raisin Sauce)

Mashed Potatoes   Giblet Gravy

Peas and Carrots   Asparagus au beurre

Cape Cod Cranberry Sauce

Hot Parker House Rolls   Butter

Mince Pie   Ice Cream   Chocolate Cake

Coffee

Apples   Salted Mixed Nuts   Oranges

Cigars   Cigarettes   Candy

1943 Thanksgiving menu.

force. Holiday routine was fine until almost 1 o'clock (P.M.) when a destroyer pulled alongside for refueling. A merchant ship needed stores as it ran out of food and it was time to turn to (that's Navy talk for time to go to work)."

Rogers makes a quick comment in his diary on November 26. "We had a wonderful dinner yesterday as you can see by the menu that is enclosed. I know this isn't a pleasant subject to talk about but I can't just get it out of my mind. I feel that I won't last out this trip. I don't know why or how I get this feeling but seems to pervade my mind. Oh well, let's forget it." On November 30 he recorded in his diary, "The weather out here is pretty rough, but the sun is shining. The ship rolls so much that it rolls us right out of bed. Otherwise, everything is okay."

The crew was always hungry for news and anxiously awaited letters from home. The ship had a post office on the starboard side forward of the crew's quarters, recalled Bruner Lange, BM2C. CMM Ed Guyer said mail was distributed on the cargo deck – some would get lots of mail and others would never receive any. Guyer's mother wrote to him seven days a week and always included a verse from the Bible. Jim Strupp, WT1C, and Louis Ragan, MOMM2C, used the mail to relay messages to their families in case one of them was seriously injured or killed. They had code words to put in letters that the family would understand, telling them what happened. Some of the ship's officers served as censors of the enlisted men's mail. Lt. j.g. Jonathan Bassett said he felt funny reading other people's mail, but it was necessary to make sure no information was being relayed that would endanger the war effort.

In November 1943, two newspapers were distributed to the crew to satisfy their hunger for news from abroad, home, and aboard the ship. The radiomen decided to put together a newspaper called *Chiwawa News*, with stories of national and international interest they got from radio transmissions received from the Associated Press and Mackay news services. This could be tricky, said Marvin Hahn, RM2C, because sometimes the signal would fade out and they only got partial stories or half the score of a ballgame. The competing paper took a more local news flavor, reporting news and events going on aboard ship. A volunteer staff of seven put together the first issue of the paper, which didn't have a name at first. In fact, across the masthead, in large letters was the word "BLANK." The staff held a contest to name the new paper, with prizes going to the top three names chosen. First prize was a carton of cigarettes, second prize one Hershey bar with almonds, and third prize a half pack of Crystomints, slightly used. The name "The Oil Spout" was chosen, but the person who submitted the name was not revealed in surviving issues of the paper.

Both papers debuted on November 30, 1943. Unfortunately, only two editions of the *Chiwawa News* survived the war years. Crew members were instructed to destroy the publication to prevent it

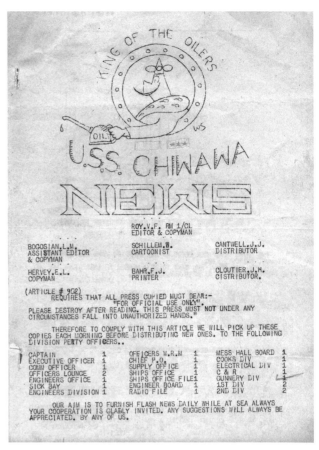

First Edition of *The Oil Spout* (aka Blank) and USS *Chiwawa News*. Both papers debuted on November 30, 1943.

from reaching enemy hands. At least eleven editions of *The Oil Spout* were produced. *The Oil Spout* covered many topics, with a catch-all section called "Pure Scuttle" reporting mischief at sea and on land along with things overheard. *The Oil Spout*'s "Ship's News" section reported on personal and professional crew events, such as promotions. All crew members were encouraged to submit stories, poetry, and anything else fit to print.

The *Chiwawa* took aboard for medical treatment T/5 Louis E. Dufour (no relation to *Chiwawa* crew member Frank Dufour) from USAT *Andrew Moore* via USS *Hobby* DD-610 by motor launch December 2. Dufour reportedly had tried to commit suicide by stabbing himself with a bayonet in the abdomen. He was taken to Norfolk and transferred to U.S. Army Hospital Fort Story for treatment on December 4. Also on December 4, the landing barges were unloaded from the cargo deck of the *Chiwawa*. The *Chiwawa* remained in Norfolk loading stores and ammunition. USS *Alcor* AR-10 was moored to the *Chiwawa* for minor repairs from December 8 through 13.

At 10 P.M. on December 3 the *Chiwawa* went to full speed of 16 knots and left the convoy without escort. On December 4 the *Chiwawa* arrived in Norfolk, Virginia. Lt. j.g. Wilton Samuel Dwyer was detached from the ship to the Naval Operating Base hospital that day for medical treatment. He died in the Naval Hospital in Norfolk on December 6, 1943. He was born on September 26, 1893, in Maine. He enlisted in the U.S. Coast Guard on April 26, 1917, and was discharged on April 1, 1919. From November 1919 to June 8, 1929, he worked on merchant ships. On August 28, 1942, he reported for active duty to the U.S. Navy to await assignment to a vessel when placed in full commission. On September 16 he was promoted to Lt. j.g., and he reported for duty to the *Chiwawa* on September 29, 1942. *The Oil Spout* edition dated December 24, 1943, had a brief memorial announcing his death. It said his nickname was "Cappy," that he was always pleasant, never spoke unkindly of anyone, and would be greatly missed. The *Chiwawa* deck log listed his next of kin contact as his mother, Mrs. Emma L. Dwyer, living in Whitman, Massachusetts.

In a December 12 letter home Rogers wrote, "Don't read my letter over a phone with a party line. You can't tell who may be listening in. This is serious. You may be costing me my life if you folks aren't careful about disclosing the contents of my letters. Don't forget dead men tell no tales so I wouldn't be able to tell you what it is like to get shot at if I am one of those that get hit. I don't mean to alarm you but please be careful who hears what I have to say in my letters."

Chapter 4
Making a Name for Itself

⚓

THE *Chiwawa* QUICKLY ESTABLISHED ITS REPUTATION FOR DELIVERing fast and efficient service in replenishing ships at sea: The crew won several competitions and the respect of the commanding officers of the ships they refueled. There was a fierce rivalry in the oiler fleet, and the *Chiwawa* became known as the *King of the Oilers*.

Ray Kern, QM2C, served on a committee that was formed to create a logo for the ship. Several designs were proposed for Cmdr. Goza to consider. One of the aspiring artists on the ship, Wallace Schillem, S1C, drew a king looking out a porthole and holding an oil can. Ray thought Schillem's "The Little King" drawing, fashioned after a cartoon character of the period, wouldn't be selected because a cartoon would be too juvenile. Ray said, "I couldn't have been more wrong. When it was shown to him [Goza], that's the one he picked out."

USS *Chiwawa* logo designed by Wallace Schillem.

Drawing taken from November 30, 1943 edition of USS *Chiwawa News*.

27

The following appeared in the first edition of *The Oil Spout* (a.k.a. Blank) dated November 30, 1943 (author unknown):

As most of the crew already knows, Schillem has drawn an insignia for the Chiwawa. This insignia portrays an old King with an oil can. It has been presented to the Captain and has met with his heartiest approval. When it is placed upon the stack, so all can see, it shall then become a challenge to each and every member of the ship's company to uphold its meaning *"King of the Oilers."*

In the short period of one year the Chiwawa has achieved a remarkable record for refueling ships at sea. At times the crew has been pressed by the handicaps of rough seas, incapable handling of ships alongside and the ever-present stand-by to stand-by that are so occurrent in the Navy. At times, delays have been caused by the bunglings of our personnel. Short though they were all must accept some small part of the blame.

These and the many trivial mistakes should be kept foremost in the minds of the guilty. A King can't afford any mistakes. The resultant emergencies caused thereby have been capably handled. From these experiences we have benefited. The old hands have increased their knowledge in the art of refueling and the new hands are in the right step. The ship as a whole has received its due praise from the Commanding Officers of the ships we refueled.

King of the Oilers is indeed a goal to achieve. One that is envied by all tankers. It is for this reason that the crew must continue on in their performance of seamanship and duty to the KING in order to uphold the tradition that we have set. This is no idle boasting for each man, deep down in his heart, is sincere in the knowledge that the Chiwawa is GOOD and the gentlemen in Washington, who keep tabs on the activities of the oilers, are aware of this fact. When asked, "What does the insignia stand for?" by some onlooker, you must answer, *"King of the Oilers."* But to answer in this way and then go on and praise the Chiwawa to the high heavens is not enough. We must prove to the fleet that the Chiwawa is the King by improving on its past performances. In this regard we must endeavor to maintain an even higher standard and strive for more efficient methods of handling the refueling operation until we have reached perfection.

Perfection is indeed what a KING justly rates and with this perfection attained our members can remind the sailors of the Fleet that they serve aboard the Chiwawa.

By the *Chiwawa's* first anniversary of delivering the goods, only 10 officers and 86 enlisted men of the commissioning crew remained aboard ship. It had attained one of the highest records of any tanker in the Atlantic service force, refueling under almost impossible conditions and surviving a concentrated submarine attack without one fatal accident.

On December 20 the *Chiwawa* left Norfolk as part of Task Unit 29.3.4 with USS *Salamonie* AO-26 and USS *Kinnebec* AO-36, escorted by USS *Badger* DD-126 and USS *Pheasant* AM-61, bound for Aruba. The crewmen wore their peacoats as they departed for the trip. Within a day, as the ship made its way south, LaVerne Rogers wrote in his diary that the temperature was rising. The ship was about 100 miles off the coast of Florida, and the men went shirtless to cope with the heat. By the next day they were carrying out their duties in shorts, and Rogers commented how funny they would look with suntans when they returned to the States. The ship arrived in Aruba on December 25. The *Chiwawa* crew loaded oil from the dock and pumped Navy Special Fuel Oil to USS *Badger*. The cooks prepared another holiday meal for the crew, similar to the Thanksgiving feast. Many of the crew recalled the weather extremes experienced on that trip – unbearable heat as they approached Aruba and then the chill as they returned to New York on January 1, 1944.

Ensign James Sherwood, who stood watch for a time as officer of the deck, said the ship's steel deck got so hot in Aruba that he laid down pieces of wood to stand on. James Veacock, Ptr2c, said the temperature reached 106 degrees. While taking depth measurements for the anchor detail, he got a severe case of sunburn and couldn't put on a coat the next week when he arrived in New York.

Many of the men decided to go into port to celebrate Christmas. "We just had a little party," said Roland Durant, s1c, though the mix of heat and alcohol proved too much to bear for some of the men. Lt. j.g. Leslie Ottman was the officer of the deck when the men returned. He said it was an incredible sight as the men staggered back to the ship. Two men who could barely walk tried to carry another who couldn't walk at all, he recalled. Lt. j.g. Ottman said the *Chiwawa* officers were invited to a Christmas party and dance at a club where Standard Oil employees were members.

LaVerne Rogers decided to explore the area and recorded the following on December 25: "So this is Aruba. What a place. Streets look like alleys in the U.S. The streets are narrow and the cars roar around at 45 miles an hour. There is no gas rationing here so the people ride around all the time. The town is nice though. All the houses are set in neat orderly rows. They have doors that run from the floor to the ceiling opening in half or all the door opens if you want it that way. I guess Mom would call them Dutch doors. That's exactly what they are. You see Aruba is in the Dutch West Indies. Most of the natives are Spanish and although they don't understand our language we got along with them very well. To get back to the houses, the houses are usually very low ceilinged and consist of two or three rooms. The doors lead on to these rooms but they were all curtained with gay colored print material. The colors here all seem to be either red or yellow. We have a few American soldiers here that know all the town and they showed us all around."

On December 27 Rogers wrote, "I have been thinking things over and I find that in two more months I have been in this Navy for a whole year and in two more months after that I will be 19. Boy am I getting old fast. I will get out of this man's Navy just two months before I turn 21."

On December 26 Task Unit 29.3.4 was reformed: uss *Salamonie* ao-26, uss *Niobrara* ao-72, and uss *Kinnebec* ao-36 escorted by uss *Badger* DD-126, uss *Pheasant* am-61, and uss *Raven* am-55. The ships arrive in New York on January 1, 1944.

On December 30 Rogers described in his diary a storm the *Chiwawa* hit about 100 miles off the northern coast of Florida, with waves so high that they were washing over the bridge. The waves broke over the bow and the spray flew over the bridge, drenching all except those in the bridge house. The storm tore loose four ready boxes loaded with ammunition. One 10-inch line spool that weighs about 400 pounds tore loose from forward of the crew's quarters and went over the side, tearing out about 15 feet of rail. The spool came back aboard aft of the crew's quarters. Several of the valves for the oil tanks were damaged and required repairs before the crew could unload oil from those tanks.

December 31, 1943, was a red-letter day for LaVerne Rogers. He told his family in his diary entry, "The paper (*The Oil Spout*) just came out and after having taken a good look at it I find that you folks will be addressing my letters wrong if you put S2c on them. From now on it shall have to be Y3c (yeoman third class). Boy, will I ever look pretty with that crow on my arm. The advancement in rate also means that I will draw a little more money. Now I shall be drawing 78 bucks instead of 64."

At 8:00 P.M. on January 6, 1944 the *Chiwawa* was one of eight oilers in convoy leaving Bayonne, New Jersey, bound for Port Arthur, Texas, to load up on oil as Task Unit 29.3.4 was reconstituted again. The *Chiwawa* was accompanied by USS *Enoree* AO-69, USS *Chicopee* AO-34, USS *Escalante* AO-70, USS *Cowanesque* AO-79, USS *Chemung* AO-30, USS *Salamonie* AO-26, and USS *Elokomin* AO-55, escorted by USS *Mosley* DE-321, USS *Vance* DE-387, USS *Pheasant* AM-61, and USS *Raven* AM-55. The group traveled in a zigzag pattern at 15 knots.

On the morning of January 7 the crew got a shocking reminder of the dangers of war. LaVerne Rogers reported in his diary on January 7, "This morning when I was on watch one of our escorts saw a couple of bodies floating by. The commodore of the convoy told this escort to pick them up. When the ship got over there they picked up 17 bodies of American seamen. The Captain mentioned that a ship was sunk out here just yesterday. That fact plus the sinking of the destroyer in New York Harbor leads me to think that there is a German sub out here having a last fling before the Allies wipe him off the map." On January 3, USS *Turner* DD-648 exploded and sank four miles southeast of Rockaway Point near Long Island, New York. The Navy's official cause of the sinking was accidental detonation of anti-submarine weapons, which killed 138 of the *Turner*'s crew.

On January 6, USS *St. Augustine* PG-54 was sunk 73 miles south-southwest of Cape May, New Jersey, after colliding with the tanker SS *Camas Meadows*. The Collision killed 115 of the *St. Augustine* crew. The *Chiwawa* arrived in Port Arthur at 9:27 P.M. on January 12. Upon entering the Sabine Pass while waiting for other ships ahead to enter the turning basin, the crew pumped out the ballast tanks too soon. With its slow speed and higher profile in the water acting like a sail, high winds pushed the ship aground near a pasture. Lt. j.g. Les Ottman recalled the surreal moment. He was standing on an oceangoing ship, gazing over the port side at cows grazing alongside. Art Krieg, SM1C, said there was a short liberty while tugs worked the ship free. He and some friends tried to sneak some booze aboard ship, but were caught and given the option to either dump it or consume it before being allowed aboard. Naturally, they retired to a shade tree and didn't waste their contraband. Also on January 12, the crew published another edition of *The Oil Spout*.

The following poem, written by Alice Rowland Kestler to Joseph Kestler, appeared in the issue.

USS *Chiwawa* – "King of the Oilers"
We're proud of our ship
and the insignia it bears
As "King of the Oilers"
On the stack up there.
We honor our Captain
whose honor has brought
A title so grand,
As seas we have crossed.
Together we won
With efforts supreme,
And together we'll continue
As King of the seas.
In storms we refueled
All ships by our side,
Handicapped by obstacles,
On the Ocean wide.
From this we've achieved
A record of skill

And challenge any ship
Who has more power or will
Our title will remain
As in the past
"King of the Oilers" –
efficient and fast.

On January 14 the *Chiwawa* left Port Arthur, bound for Norfolk escorted by USS *Vance* DE-387. The trip was uneventful, except on January 17 when planes from Miami flew above them all day. Two suspicious ships were spied on the horizon and the crew was called to general quarters, but nothing came of it, Rogers reported in his diary. The *Chiwawa* arrived in Norfolk at 11:59 P.M. January 19.

On January 25 the *Chiwawa* departed for Casablanca in Convoy UGS-31. Along with its usual cargo of kerosene, diesel oil, and fuel oil for the escort destroyers, the ship also carried airplane motors upon its cargo deck. Sailors and pilots were also along for the ride to join the fight. On January 26 the Allies attempted to establish another beachhead in Italy about 30 miles south of Rome at Anzio – code named "Operation Shingle." LaVerne Rogers reported 104 ships in the convoy (the biggest convoy the ship had participated in to date) and lamented in his January 25 diary entry that he had missed his high school graduation ceremony. He also reported in his January 28 diary entry that due to some of the broken-down old hulks in the convoy they were only able to make 9 knots.

On February 1, LaVerne Rogers described the rough seas. "The waves are so high that when the ship rolls over too far the sea rushes over our decks. It's a pretty sight to see blue water rush over the deck and break up into small drips that have a light blue color to them." On February 2 Rogers reported that at 8 P.M. the ship would be halfway to its destination, having traveled 700 miles. Also on February 2 the *Chiwawa* dropped astern of the convoy to refuel USS *Dupont* DD-162, USS *George E. Badger* DD-196, USS *Clemson* DD-186, and USS *Osmond Ingram* DD-255. The *Chiwawa* rejoined the convoy later that evening. Rogers said in his February 3 diary entry that one of the escorts had a sub contact (by radar), but nothing came of it. On February 4 the *Chiwawa* dropped astern of the convoy again to exercise gunnery practice. On February 9 the *Chiwawa* detached from the convoy with three merchant ships, escorted by USS *Badger*, USS *Clemson* and USS *Dupont*. The group heads directly for Casablanca. On February 9 Rogers reported in his diary, "A mine floated through the convoy but it didn't touch a single ship although it came mighty near one of the destroyers. It was warned in time and moved out of the way. The commodore of the convoy wouldn't let any of the cans sink it though. Puzzling isn't it. That mine is a menace to navigation." Arriving in Casablanca on February 10 Rogers tells his diary, "We landed in Casablanca this afternoon about 1400 (2 P.M.). The place looked the same from what we could see. A merchant ship had been sunk in the harbor last night. A torpedo hit it in the bow and the ship is grounded with three-fourths of it sticking above the water." During their stay in Casablanca the commander of the destroyers in the convoy threw a beer party. *The Oil Spout* reported that several divisions of the ship spent time on the beach playing softball against each other. The crew members were also challenged by a team from the USS *Badger*. The *Chiwawa* defeated them 13-5. Frank Ward, Lewis Miehlke, and Clayton Sheppy all took turns on the pitcher's mound. *The Oil Spout* reported that a work detail of Italian POWs was brought aboard, to the great delight of the *Chiwawa*'s crew members of Italian extraction.

Convoy GUS-30, consisting of 68 merchant ships plus 14 escort ships and the *Chiwawa*, left Casablanca for Norfolk on February 16. Aboard the *Chiwawa* was the precious cargo of mail that carried news from soldiers and sailors to their families on the home front. The convoy encountered bad weather from February 22 to March 3. On February 25 the *Chiwawa* refueled the destroyers USS *George E. Badger*, USS *Osmond Ingram*, USS *Clemson*, and USS *Dupont* in two-and-a-half hours. "Darn good even for the Chiwawa," noted Rogers in his diary. On February 29 the *Chiwawa* refueled USS *Dupont*, USS *Badger*, and USS *Clemson*. Stormy weather and a broken fuel hose cut short the *Chiwawa*'s refueling operations for the day. Rogers reported in his diary on March 3 that the ship was tossed about in an 11-degree roll. He also said the weather delayed the ship's arrival in Norfolk by five days, which sunk the men's spirits. They traveled 188 miles from noon on March 3 to noon on March 4. The *Chiwawa* arrived in Norfolk on March 8 after spending 21 days at sea. The *Chi-*

wawa discharged its black oil cargo to the dock and spent the next month in dry dock for maintenance and Navy yard work.

During this time some of the crew took time for leave or liberty and found some mischief. While the "Kings of the Oilers" were making a name for themselves, sometimes they made mistakes – as the deck log revealed. William "Big Rebel" Rhinehardt (at the time MM1c) was court-martialed for unjustifiable violence. Jim Strupp, WT1c, thinks he vaguely recalled the circumstances of the incident. Jim said "Big Rebel" was an incredibly big, strong, and agile man who loved to fight. He recalled a bar fight in which Rhinehardt grabbed two men by the back of the neck, slammed their heads together, and nearly killed both of them.

Chapter 5
The Invasion of Europe

⚓

WITH THE INVASION OF EUROPE AT HAND, THE RESTED AND READY *Chiwawa* crew set out from the Navy yard at Norfolk unescorted on April 5, 1944, to stock up on black oil and gasoline at Beaumont and Port Arthur, Texas. The *Chiwawa* arrived in Port Arthur on April 10. The *Chiwawa* departed Beaumont on April 13 and returned to Norfolk on April 18. Departing Norfolk on April 21, the *Chiwawa* brought oil and 37 Army personnel to Bermuda, escorted by the mine sweeper USS *Implicit* AM-246, which was on its first cruise. The *Chiwawa* arrived in St. George on April 23. After unloading black oil and gasoline the ship departed St. George on April 26, escorted by USS *Implicit*, and arrived in New York on April 28. By May 1, 1944, only eight of the 24 officers and 64 of 188 enlisted men that commissioned the ship were still attached to the *Chiwawa*.

On May 5, the *Chiwawa* departed New York bound for Belfast, Ireland, with Task Group 27.10. The *Chiwawa* deck log mentioned one ammunition ship, one mine layer, one cruiser, and nine destroyers sailed with the *Chiwawa*. On May 8, the *Chiwawa* refueled nine destroyers and the mine layer. The task group arrived in Belfast just before midnight on May 14. Many of the task force ships assembled with other ships in the area in preparation for the Normandy invasion. Some fired on the beaches during the invasion. While in Belfast the *Chiwawa* also refueled USS *Texas* BB-35, which fired on Normandy beach on D-Day. The *Chiwawa* then headed off to Glasgow, Scotland, and rewarded some of the crew with a short liberty.

The *Chiwawa* started its return trip to New York on May 19 in Convoy UTC-23, arriving there on May 28. The convoy of 40 ships was escorted by one cruiser and 13 destroyer escorts. The voyage was uneventful, except for the discovery of a dead German sailor in the water by the crew of USS *Lee Fox* DE-65 on May 21. He was nicknamed "Herman the German" with no malice by the *Lee Fox* crew. Everett Schrader, SOM1C, of the USS *Ira Jeffrey* DE-63, later obtained a diary from an officer of the *Lee Fox* revealing that "Herman" was from U-473, which was sunk on May 6, 1944, by depth charges from British sloops HMS *Starling*, HMS *Wren*, and HMS *Wild Goose*. There were 24 dead and 30 survivors. The dead German wore a green uni-

17 May 1944.

INFORMATION FOR LIBERTY PARTY

1. Liberty will commence at about 1400 this date.. Uniform - Dress Blues - White hat.

2. English money will be exchanged for American money in Supply Office prior to departure of liberty party.

3. Liberty launch will land at Gourock Pier. Trains leave Gourock for Glasgow at 1435, 1600, 1630, and 1700. A train also leaves at 1520 but it is necessary to change trains in Port Glasgow.

4. Liberty party will NOT return to ship in its present location. Liberty party will meet the ship at Dunglass Docks, Bowling. The only way to get to Bowling is by bus or train from Glasgow.

5. All liberty party will assemble at Waterloo Bus Station, Glasgow prior to 2100. It is imperative that all men be there at this time in the event they may be notified of any change in orders.

6. At Waterloo Bus Station, liberty party will take orders from a Ship's Officer who will be on hand at that time.

7. Money may also be exchanged in limited quantities at American Red Cross, Glasgow.

Information for Liberty Party visiting Scotland dated May 17, 1944.

Ray Kern, QM2C, celebrates his Scottish heritage by posing in a kilt.

form and an escape lung of the type used in exiting a submerged submarine. He was a Matroseengefreiter (able seaman) named Albert Buddendiock, and his parents lived in Warstein, Sauerland, Germany. The body had floated with the ocean current 147 miles when he was found. An autopsy estimated his age to be 18 to 20 years of age and revealed he had died of exhaustion, not drowning. The man's military papers and personal letters from home (which included a field post number bearing the identity of the U-boat) were turned over to Naval Intelligence. He was buried at sea with full military honors.

Also during the convoy, USS *Frament* DE-677 made a sound contact with German subs and fired 24 hedgehogs (depth charges with a total of 1,500 pounds of TNT) that exploded upon hitting bottom at 50 fathoms.

With their arrival in New York on May 28 the ship's crew spent the next week in the Big Apple. They celebrated with a party and dance at the Ritz Carlton Hotel on June 1 and 2 – the event was paid for with funds from the ship's store. *The Oil Spout* reported that the King of the Oilers crew lived up to its reputation once again as everyone had a good time and managed to stay within the bounds of propriety. Some had plans to go but didn't make it.

Robert Schellenberger, WT2c, and his girlfriend, Ada, got into an argument in an ice cream parlor the afternoon before the dance. Robert said, "If you weren't so stubborn, maybe I'd take you to a dance tonight." Ada snapped back, "Maybe if you weren't so stupid, I'd go." The couple later married.

Lt. Edward O'Neill headed a committee that provided the dance hall, food, and beverages. The crew and its guests danced to the music of a live band. A conga line formed that trailed into the street. CBM James Spence took second place in a jitterbug contest. His version of the dance included a mixture of Continental Rhumba and an Irish Jig. Other dancers of note were Russell "Rusty" Berman, Y2c, and Edmund "Shorty" Correira, GM1c. The evening ended early for some like Ken Wood, Cox, and his girlfriend, Myrna, who was a nurse. They attended the dance on June 1. She had a midnight curfew to be in the Nurse's Residence in Brooklyn. Art Krieg, SM1c, and three of his *Chiwawa* friends had such a good time that they overslept the next morning and nearly missed the ship as the crew prepared for the next convoy. They arrived at the dock as the ship was leaving port. As a quick-thinking signalman, Art got onto a Coast Guard ship and sent a message via signal light to the *Chiwawa* to stop and let them come aboard. The motor launch was sent out to pick them up. Art said Cmdr. Goza made him write something 100 times, like a school kid's punishment.

The *Chiwawa* departed New York with Convoy CU-27 on June 8. The *Chiwawa*'s cargo consisted of gasoline, black oil (a type of navy fuel oil), diesel oil, and fourteen sailors for transport to USS *Susan B. Anthony* AP-72. That ship sank on June 7, 1944 after hitting a mine while carrying reinforcements to Omaha Beach. The convoy consisted of six U.S. cargo ships, twelve U.S. tankers, two U.S. oilers, one British cargo ship, one Norwegian cargo ship, and two British escort aircraft carriers, escorted by six U.S. destroyer escorts. The convoy encountered beautiful, sunny weather from June 8-11. On June 12 the weather turned overcast with rain and fog. Also on June 12 the *Chiwawa* refueled USS *Sims* DE-154, USS *Griffin* DE-54, USS *Lawrence* DE-53, and USS *Hopping* DE-155. On June 13 the *Chiwawa* refueled USS *Reeves* DE-156. On June 14 the *Chiwawa* crew held firing practice with its 40mm and 3-inch guns. The convoy arrived in Loch Long, Scotland, on June 20. The fourteen sailors were transferred to USS *Susan B. Anthony*.

On June 21 the *Chiwawa* moved to Bowling, Scotland, to discharge some of its cargo. The ship began its return trip to the United States just before midnight on June 23 with Convoy UC-27. The convoy consisted of nine U.S. cargo ships, 13 U.S. tankers, three British cargo ships, and two U.S. oilers, including the *Chiwawa*. Six U.S. destroyer escorts and two British escort carriers escorted the convoy. Also traveling with the convoy was HMS *Nelson*, a British battleship, which was heading to Philadelphia, Pennsylvania, for repairs after hitting two mines on June 18, 1944, while supporting the Normandy invasion. On July 1, the *Chiwawa* refueled USS *Charles Lawrence* DE-53 and USS *Sims* DE-154. In the morning of July 3 the *Chiwawa*, USS *Winooski* AO-38, and HMS *Arbiter*, with USS *Sims* as escort, left the convoy and headed to Norfolk. The rest of the convoy went to New York. The *Chiwawa* arrived in Norfolk on July 4. William Delfert, RM3c, noted in his diary that the *Chiwawa* had traveled 3,120 miles during the convoy. The men had ten days until the next convoy and the *Chiwawa* had routine overhaul and repair work done. Many of them took advantage of the time for leave. Some men, including CGM Francis Charles Clouse, were transferred to other ships. Clouse was later killed in action. He is the only former *Chiwawa* crewman known to have died in combat.

Clouse was born on a family farm near Foxholm, North Dakota, on November 20, 1920. He was the tenth child of thirteen children born to William and Juliana (Haider) Clouse. He spent his childhood helping with farm chores and attending school in Foxholm.

Fascinated by stories of Navy life related to him by friends and family, Francis eagerly joined the Navy on December 20, 1937. He spent four years on USS *Idaho* BB-42 and served as an instructor at Naval Operating Base, Norfolk,

CGM Francis C. Clouse 1920–1945

Virginia. He reenlisted on November 2, 1942. He was then assigned to the *Chiwawa* on December 24, 1942, making him a plank owner.

He was popular among the crew and was regular Navy, Art Krieg, SM1c, recalled. He was also remembered for the well-maintained beards he grew. His younger sisters remembered how he would come home from training and practice marching them around the farmyard. He achieved the rank of Chief Gunners Mate on May 1, 1944. He was separated from the *Chiwawa* on July 13 and sent to the Navy yard in Washington, D.C. for Gunner's Mate and Electric Hydraulic Instruction.

He was assigned to USS *Hugh W. Hadley* DD-774 in time for its commissioning on November 25, 1944. The destroyer was sent to Okinawa, reaching the port on April 1, 1945. Francis, 24, was killed during an attack by the Japanese on May 11, 1945, in which the *Hadley* took three kamikaze hits. He was hit by a flying piece of debris while standing next to a torpedo tube on the starboard side. He was buried at sea. A citation was given to the family for his bravery in service to his country. It reads in part:

"When the USS *Hadley was seriously damaged during heavy Japanese air attack off Okinawa, Clouse took a hose and rushed to the section of the ship set afire by the hit. Although in danger from exploding ammunition and extensive fires, he kept the blaze under control until he was mortally wounded by the crash of an enemy suicide plane near his station."*

Art Krieg said Francis put in for a transfer because he wanted to see more action. Art also said that when they got the news Francis had been killed they knew he went down with his guns blazing. CGM Francis C. Clouse was awarded the following medals and awards: American Defense Medal, American Campaign Medal, European African Middle Eastern Campaign Medal (one Battle Star), Asia Pacific Campaign Medal (one Battle Star), Combat Action Ribbon, Presidential Unit Citation, Navy Good Conduct Medal, World War II Victory Medal, Bronze Star (posthumously) and Purple Heart (posthumously). He gave all his tomorrows for your today.

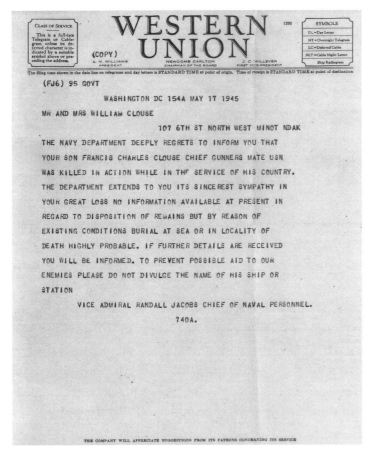

Telegram received by the Clouse Family announcing Francis's death.

The *Chiwawa* left Norfolk with Convoy UGS-48 on July 14. The convoy consisted of forty-six U.S. cargo ships, two U.S. tankers, four U.S. Navy oilers, nine British cargo ships, eight British tankers, and two Norwegian tankers. The *Chiwawa*'s cargo was Navy Special Fuel Oil, diesel oil, lubricating oil in drums, six MK VI depth charges, and 19 sailors as passengers for transport. On July 17 the convoy participated in a simulated air attack from friendly carrier planes.

Many ships had problems breaking down during the voyage. On July 23 SS *Empire Ragoon* straggled 50 miles behind the convoy and USS *Buckley* DE-51 stayed with her. The convoy encountered rain and mist all day on July 25, with the weather improving on July 26. On July 27 rough seas slowed the convoy. The USS *Ruben James* DE-153 had a sound contact on July 29 and dropped 13 depth charges, though the suspect sub later proved to be fish. The *Chiwawa* arrived in Mers El Kebir, Algeria, on July 30 without incident, traveling 3,590 miles according to William Delfert's log. The rest of the convoy continued on to Bizerte, Tunisia. German planes attacked the convoy before it reached its destination. On July 31 the *Chiwawa* moored in Mers El Kebir alongside USS *Cowanesque* AO-79 while taking on a fresh load of black oil and cargo that included 23 MK VI depth charges, mine-sweeping gear, and 400 smoke pots. The *Chiwawa* departed for its next big mission in Naples, Italy, on the morning of August 3 as one of the supply ships for the invasion of Southern France. The mission was code named Operation "Anvil." Traveling with USS *Winooski* AO-38, USS *Davis* DE-136, and USS *Herbert E. Jones* DE-137, the crew kept its defensive skills sharp with general quarter drills and anti-aircraft target practice in which the ship's gunners fired at balloons.

James Veacock, Ptr2c, said the Mediterranean water was beautiful. He recalled dolphins swimming alongside the ship. Just before the quartet of ships arrived in Naples, USS *Winooski* AO-38 left the group for another destination. The remaining ships arrived in Naples on August 5. The area around Naples was heavily damaged from the fighting and from sabotage as German forces withdrew from the city. Mount Vesuvius had erupted the previous March.

Crew interviews described Naples as a bombed-out and dirty city with poor and hungry citizens. Even with little to eat for themselves Harry Baynes, Cox, said he was invited to a spaghetti dinner with a local family. Mike Pfister, GM1C, said he attended Mass in a bombed-out church with his shipmates.

Many of the *Chiwawa* crew had to report to sick bay to be vaccinated before they could go ashore as the *Chiwawa's* written daily routine for August 10, 1944, revealed that Bradford Hosmer, EM3C, shared for researching this book. Lt. j.g. Leslie Ottman said most of the area around the port was bombed out.

Art Krieg (left) and Bill Hall in Naples, Italy on August 27, 1944.

The tourist attractions were open for business, though, and many of the crew took time to see Pompeii and the ancient ruins. Nights were always in blackout condition so there was little point in nighttime excursions, said Lt. j.g. Leslie Ottman. Many of the crewmen caught up with relatives who were in the Army while on R and R in Naples. Jim Strupp, WT1C, said one of the most beautiful things he ever saw was Mount Vesuvius from the ocean. Lt. j.g. Leslie Ottman added that the sunrise looked like it was coming right out of the crater's mouth – a breathtaking sight. The enemy still lurked in the area, and German observation planes flew over almost every evening. The planes came to be dubbed "Washing Machine Charlie" as Warren Ray, MM2C, remembered. Jim Strupp, WT1C, also recalled the ship was not allowed to fire at them, and a smokescreen was put up. The smoke was so thick you thought you were going to choke to death as shore batteries opened up on the planes, he recalled.

Soon after arrival, the *Chiwawa's* crew refueled ships from the United States, United Kingdom, Greece, and Italy as part of Task Force 80.7. The *Chiwawa* earned a second battle star on its European African Middle Eastern Campaign Ribbon for its part in Operation "Anvil."

With its mission completed, the *Chiwawa* left Naples on August 31, escorted by USS *Parker* DD-604 stopping in Oran, Algeria on September 2 to deliver black oil and deck cargo. On September 4 the *Chiwawa* left Oran bound for Norfolk in convoy with USS

Texas BB-35, USS *Arkansas* BB-33, USS *Nevada* BB-36, USS *Pinto* ATF-90 and Destroyer Squadron 16, consisting of USS *Parker* DD-604, USS *Boyle* DD-600, USS *Champlin* DD-601, USS *Ordronaux* DD-617, and USS *Nields* DD-616 as escort. The *Chiwawa* refueled four destroyers on September 8. On September 13 the *Chiwawa* received word of a hurricane approaching Norfolk and received orders to report to New York. The ship arrived in New York on September 14 traveling 3,610 miles, according to a log kept by William Delfert, RM3c.

Chapter 6
Turning the Tide

⚓

WITH THE ENEMY ON THE RUN ON BOTH FRONTS, THE *Chiwawa* arrived in New York on September 14, 1944, giving the crew some time for R and R. The evening of September 14 was a memorable one for Clyde Clark, EM3c. One of his duties as an electrician's mate involved fixing electrical items that broke down aboard ship. On that night the captain's refrigerator broke, and he was called to repair it. The ship was encountering rough seas, and while making his way back from the captain's quarters to get some tools, he grabbed the side of a hatch to steady himself. The wind closed the watertight door, slamming it on his hands. He said he didn't even notice his finger was smashed until someone stopped him and pointed out that something was dripping. He looked down and, seeing blood, nearly fainted. The ship's physician, Dr. Harry L. Allan, Jr., treated him and amputated the fourth finger at the first joint on his right hand. Clyde received no disability from the government, which claimed he wasn't disabled. He added, "You try to open a pair of pliers without that fingertip and then tell me I wasn't disabled."

While on leave, some of the crew managed to put the war aside and plan for the future. Ensign (later Lt. j.g.) Jonathan Bassett proposed marriage to his girlfriend, Sigrid Dorothy "Dot" Edwards by letter in August 1944. To get around the censors he referred to the scheduled date of the ship's arrival in Norfolk as a certain number of days from her birthday, October 23. During the trip back from Oran the convoy was diverted to New York due to a hurricane making its way up the coast from the Caribbean. This actually worked to their advantage as the wedding was to be held in New York. But Jonathan had no idea if his proposal was accepted because the responding letter was waiting in Norfolk. He arrived in New York and went to Dot's home to find a room full of clothes. His soon to be mother-in-law chased him out of the house because they were in the process of putting together Dot's trousseau. The edge of the hurricane hit New York just before the wedding, knocking out the power. Dot's mother called the Navy to get power restored because her daughter was marrying a Navy man. Power was restored in time for the wedding. Dot's father was a longshoreman and had connections to secure plenty of the best food and top-shelf alcohol for the special occasion. Friends and relatives came from New York, New Jersey, Pennsylvania, and Connecticut.

They were married on September 23 in Annadale Lutheran Church on Staten Island. Shipmates Lt. j.g. Martin Marquard and Lt. j.g. James Connelly were in the wedding party. The reception was at Dot's aunt's house in Annadale and the wedding night was spent at the Astor Hotel in Times Square. The couple traveled by train to New Haven and then took a bus to East River, Connecticut, to spend the rest of the honeymoon with the Bassett family. Jonathan's uncle loaned them his car while they were there.

Wedding party: Irene Lorsen (left), Betty Bassett, Ruth Hall, Sigrid Bassett, Jon Bassett, Philip Bassett, James Connelly, and Martin Marquard.

Martin Marquard (left) and Lester Gawlocki visit with Sigrid Bassett at her wedding reception.

On September 16 the *Chiwawa* began to unload its cargo of black oil and diesel oil to the dock. On September 17 the *Chiwawa* underwent routine overhaul and repair. Many of the crew went on leave.

For the young men of the crew, life was filled with a lot of uncertainty. Liberties and leaves – a welcome release from the boredom of the daily routine at sea – were cancelled on short notice.

Most of the crew had no idea where they were or where they were going. This was especially true for the "snipes," as the men working the fire room and engine room were sometimes called. The joke was that these crewmen wanted submarine pay because they worked below the waterline. "The only way we had any idea which way we were going was the quartermaster strikers came around changing the clocks frequently, which meant we were going east-west. And if they didn't change the clocks we were going north-south," remembered Jim Strupp, wt1c. Every time the *Chiwawa* left the States fully loaded with oil there were no guarantees they would ever see home again. Life had a different meaning with ever-present danger, and the crew lived life to the fullest. Jim Strupp remembered the routine each time the crew arrived in New York or Norfolk: "When we arrived in the States the first thing was getting paid. Then you went

Ed Guyer (left), Louis Ragan, James Strupp and Warren Ray take time to celebrate with friends in Times Square, New York in September 1944.

somewhere to get a haircut, shower, and your uniform pressed. Then you went out on the town to the best restaurants. We never waited in line as long as we were in uniform," Jim remembered. Of course, being young and full of spunk did lead to its share of mischief and trouble as the deck log and many crew interviews revealed.

With R and R complete, the *Chiwawa* and its crew returned to the job of delivering the goods. On October 2 the ship left New York, escorted by USS *Whipple* DD-217, bound for Bermuda with black oil, gasoline, and sailors with orders for new assignments. Arriving on October 4 the crew delivered oil to several dock locations and gasoline to the Naval Air Station. There was time available for liberty and some of the crew volunteered for shore patrol duty. The ship departed Bermuda on October 7 bound for Aruba, with USS *Whipple* as an escort. While en route, the crew held target practice with 20mm and 40mm guns to test their marksmanship. Arriving in Aruba on October 11 the crew loaded black oil and gasoline aboard the *Chiwawa*. The ship departed the next day bound for Guantanamo Bay, Cuba, with USS *Whipple* as escort. While en route the 3-inch guns got their chance at target practice, shooting at star shells. The crew delivered the ship's cargo upon arrival in Guantanamo Bay on October 14.

The *Chiwawa* left Cuba on October 18 bound for Texas City, Texas, with USS *Whipple* as escort. Once again, the crew conducted general quarters drills and performed surface-target practice, firing the 3-inch, 5-inch and 40mm guns. The ship arrived in Texas City on October 22, completing the 1,273-mile journey from Cuba. The *Chiwawa* loaded 69,812 barrels of black oil in an eight-hour period. On October 23 the crew loaded another 32,950 barrels of gasoline in an eight-hour period before departing for Norfolk, with USS *Whipple* as escort.

On October 26 the radio room published the news from home and from the front lines of the war. Thomas Kovach, GM2c, saved a copy of the publication among his souvenirs. Using a typical zigzag pattern and traveling at a speed of 15.5 knots, the *Chiwawa* arrived in its home port on October 29, concluding a 2,800-mile trip. Upon arrival, it was business as usual. There was a transfer of crew, and the crew loaded aboard general stores, diesel oil, and drums of lubricating oil.

Joining the Navy was the first experience away from home for many of the young crew, and it gave them their first opportunity to experience parts of the country and the world they had never before seen. Frank Dufour (then S1c) had been on the ship 17 months when he wrote to his younger sister, Marie, in Philadelphia on October 27, 1944, "Well kid, we are on our way to Norfolk. I guess we will be in tomorrow some time. I did not get liberty in Texas and I sure

was disappointed because there sure are a lot of pretty girls down there. We were only there a day and a half. Is it ever rough right now. I can hardly write this letter. The waves are coming clean over the ship. We are under the water more than we are on top. The ship is rolling all over the place. Hope you could get a ride like this. I'll bet you would not want another one. I can just see you now sick as the devil and heaving over the rail. Did you receive my letter from Texas? I hope so. I

Frank Dufour, Cox.

guess you know kid, I am getting around a little. If I ever get married and have enough money to spend a honeymoon I am going to spend it in Cuba. That sure is a nice place. Even nicer than Bermuda. Hope you get down there one of these days."

November 1944 proved to be a month filled with many challenges. Convoy UGS-59 left Norfolk bound for Casablanca on November 1. The convoy consisted of 89 ships escorted by one U.S. destroyer, eight U.S. destroyer escorts, and one French escort ship. The average speed of the convoy was 8.81 knots, and the convoy encountered some rough seas during the trip. The *Chiwawa*'s cargo was kerosene, diesel oil, lubricating oil in drums, and four U.S. Navy officers for transport to new assignments on U.S. Navy destroyers. At 6 P.M. on November 8 the *Chiwawa*'s crew received word from SS *Duncan U. Fletcher* that one of the Armed Guard, Donald Murray, S1C, was seriously ill. From the symptoms, the *Chiwawa*'s newly appointed medical officer, Dr. John P. Coughlin, diagnosed acute appendicitis. The case was reported to the Escort Commander in USS *Nields* DD-616. At 6:30 P.M. the *Chiwawa* received instructions to fall astern of the convoy with SS *Duncan U. Fletcher* and USS *Pride* DE-323 to attempt transfer of the patient by *Chiwawa*'s 40-foot motor launch. The operation began at 7:28 P.M., with SS *Duncan U. Fletcher* approaching on the port side as the ships slowed to a speed of three knots while preparing the motor launch for transfer of the patient in turbulent waters. At 8:32 P.M. guy to beam parted. At 9:05 P.M. there was another attempt to launch the motor launch, and at 9:10 P.M. the motor launch's hull punctured as it swayed against the port rail. The operation was aborted due to the increasing sea and swell and the damage to the motor launch. The Escort Commander ordered the three ships to remain together and to resume the patient transfer in daylight. The three ships increased speed to 11.5 knots to keep up with the convoy. At 8:34 A.M. on November 9 a breeches buoy was sent over to SS *Duncan U. Fletcher* and the patient was transferred to the *Chiwawa* at 8:40 A.M. The diagnosis was confirmed and the appendicitis had become gangrenous. The doctor performed surgery at 11:10 A.M. and the patient was expected to make a full recovery.

Donald Bulger, AERM3C, remembered well the attempt to lower the large motor launch over the port side of the ship during rough seas. He had watched as the launch smashed into the ship's hull during heavy rolling. Bulger also remembered the several attempts to fire the lead line over to the merchant ship to haul the breeches line to that ship. Members of the crew saw sparks fly from the merchant ship's hull as it rolled before the line was successfully hauled in. Members of the *Chiwawa* crew held the line, taking in and playing out slack as the two ships rolled. It took time waiting for the ships to roll in some sort of synchronism to control the transfer.

The rough seas made the patient transfer especially difficult because the ships were tossed about like corks. Once the motor launch was out of the cradle, it would swing out and slam against the side of the ship with every swell. Frank Dufour, a coxswain on the motor launch, said, "It was a good thing we never made it into the water because we would have been goners for sure. The water was so rough that night the waves were a wall of water that would have swamped us for sure." Once the operation was aborted, the next problem was to recover the men from the motor launch. Each time the motor launch swung towards the ship a couple of sailors would jump back onto the ship. It was a very frightening experience for everyone involved. Louis Ragan, momm2c, was visibly scared as he relayed his story to Jim Strupp, wt1c, in the fire room.

Ensign Elliott Royce said he witnessed a heated argument on the bridge between Cmdr. John P. Goza and executive officer Lt. Cmdr. George V. Sargent as to whether the operation should be aborted before the motor launch was wrecked. Goza reportedly said that the operation had to go forward: "We got to go! We got to go!" but Sargent reportedly said he wanted to wait for calmer seas and daylight. Sargent said, "Every man has two hands. One hand for himself and one hand for the Navy."

After transferring the patient, the ships returned to the convoy and the normal duties of delivering the goods. Rough seas continued to plague the convoy, and several of the *Chiwawa*'s crewmen were injured during refueling because strong waves knocked them against stanchions and hoses. On November 13 the *Chiwawa* accepted another sailor in need of medical attention. Gasper Titone, BM2c, was transferred by breeches buoy from uss *Burke* DE-215 for treatment of a skin infection on his right hand.

The stress of being on an oiler – with constant u-boat alerts and other dangers – took its toll on the mental well-being of some of the crew. The deck log revealed several cases of treatment for mental problems throughout the war. Some crew members recalled, for example, that Earl W. Rauser, MM1c, exhibited strange behavior and seemed to have trouble coping with the stress of war. To keep his mind occupied, they put him on a cleaning and rat-catching detail. The men in the engine room and fire room knew his condition was getting worse, but thought he was harmless. On November 13, 1944, the situation came to a head when Rauser attempted to attack a sleeping sailor with a ball-peen hammer. Luckily, the sailor being attacked wrestled the hammer away from Rauser before any harm was done. By order of Dr. Coughlin, Rauser was taken to sick bay for safekeeping, where he was stripped of his clothes and reportedly showed signs of schizophrenia. CBM Al Anton was assigned sick bay guard duty to ensure that Rauser stayed there. Unfortunately, Al didn't watch closely enough and Rauser escaped through a porthole, and ran to the fantail of the ship. Art Krieg, SM1c, who was coming off his watch at that moment, recalled his surprise when he saw Al Anton carrying a fire ax and chasing a naked man across the length of the ship. Rauser made it to the rear of the ship and climbed up the stack. Dr. Coughlin was called aft to assist. He looked up and said, "When he gets hungry, he'll come down." After several hours Rauser came down and he was put in the brig for detention until the ship's arrival in port.

Over the next couple of days more sailors were transferred to the *Chiwawa* for medical attention. They later returned to their ships. On November 15 two destroyer escort ships went astern of the convoy for refueling with the *Chiwawa* and simultaneously loaded them with Navy Special Fuel Oil. In two hours and 15 minutes the crew delivered 39,018 gallons to USS *Enright* DE-216 and 39,858 gallons to USS *Scott* DE-214. The same evening, the *Chiwawa*'s crew returned a patient to USS *Burke* after he received treatment, and the *Chiwawa*'s crew delivered 43,974 gallons of Navy Special Fuel Oil to that ship as well. The *Chiwawa* also loaded USS *Nields* DD-616 with 50,274 gallons of Navy Special Fuel Oil. An electrical short circuit triggered a small fire in the *Chiwawa*'s #2 3-inch gun, and the fire was quickly extinguished with minimal damage. The crew took some target practice with 20mm and 40mm guns on November 17. The convoy finally arrived in Casablanca late that evening and delivered its remaining cargo of diesel oil and Navy Special Fuel Oil the next morning. The *Chiwawa* had traveled 3,439 miles from Norfolk to Casablanca according to William Delfert's log.

Some sailors volunteered for shore patrol. Jim Strupp, WT1C, said volunteering for shore patrol was a good way to log in some sightseeing, so he volunteered for the opportunity in Casablanca. An officer handed him a .45 semi-automatic pistol. Jim noticed it had no shells and asked, "Where are the shells for this?" To which the officer replied, "You don't need any." Jim had shot target pistol and rifle before the war, and he was not going into a potentially dangerous situation with an unloaded gun. He handed back the pistol and said, "Then I un-volunteer if you're going to send me into some place with an empty gun." The officer promptly found some shells and Jim left for shore patrol.

Jim Strupp (left), William Davis, and Francis Dugan perform shore patrol duty in Casablanca.

On November 20 the *Chiwawa* moved to Fadala, French Morocco, to deliver more of its cargo, and returned to Casablanca the next day. On November 24 the *Chiwawa* began its return trip to Norfolk in convoy GUS-59. The convoy consisted of 97 ships escorted by one U.S. destroyer and seven U.S. destroyer escorts. The *Chiwawa* transported 23 sailors as passengers. On November 28 the *Chiwawa* refueled the USS *Weber* DE-675, USS *Schmidt* DE-676, and USS *Selfridge* DD-357 with a total of 88,116 gallons of Navy Special Fuel Oil in three hours. The crew participated in general quarters drills and took target practice with the port 40mm and 5-inch gun on November 29. The crew celebrated Thanksgiving November 30 with a large dinner. At that time, only four officers and 50 enlisted men of the commissioning crew remained attached to the *Chiwawa*.

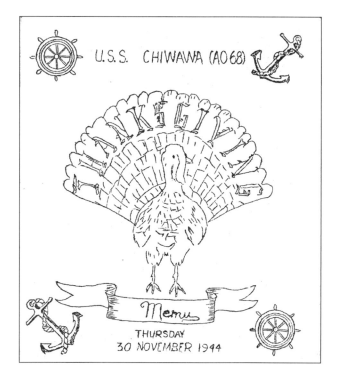

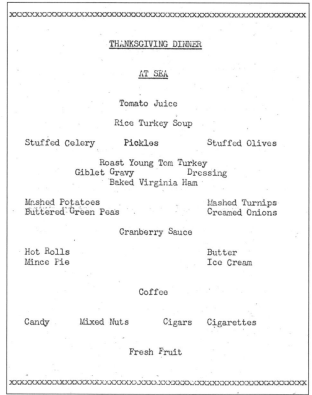

Thanksgiving 1944 menu.

On December 1 the convoy was well into its voyage and the escort ships were hungry for fuel. The *Chiwawa* delivered 86,604 gallons of Navy Special Fuel Oil to destroyer escorts USS *Weber* DE-675, USS *Schmitt* DE-676, USS *Mosley* DE-321, USS *Newell* DE-322, USS *Lowe* DE-325, USS *Falgout* DE-324, and USS *Pride* DE-323 in an eight-hour period. On December 2 and 3 the *Chiwawa* delivered spare radar parts to USS *Newell*. The convoy arrived safely in Norfolk on December 10 without incident. While proceeding up the channel to the Navy yard the next day, the *Chiwawa* narrowly escaped a collision with *LSM-280*. The LSM approached on the wrong side of the channel and attempted to cross from starboard to port. The *Chiwawa*'s crew sounded the danger signal and turned the engines full astern. With the danger gone, the *Chiwawa* proceeded to the Navy Yard dry dock for repairs.

Frank Dufour, S1C, wrote to his sister, Marie, in Philadelphia on December 11, 1944, "You're not kidding the days go fast. Just think, in two more months I will be twenty (he would turn 20 on February 23, 1945). Getting old. It won't be long til I'm a man." At the time, Frank had been in the Navy 19 months and had visited African, European, and Caribbean ports.

Frank also wrote to Marie on December 18, 1944: "Oh, by the way kid you ought to see the mustache I am raising. I had it for about four or five months now. It sure is a beauty. Like Clark Gable's."

With the holiday season in full swing, many of the crew went on leave to spend time with family and friends. Many thought the war's end in Europe was near. Those thoughts were quickly abandoned when the Germans began a counter-offensive on December 16 along a 60-mile front in France. Catching the Allies completely by surprise, this offensive became known as the Battle of the Bulge. On December 17, the *Chiwawa* left dry dock to prepare to make an attempt to help the retreating Allies with a fuel delivery. On the same day, a spark from a welder's torch set a flag bag on fire on the *Chiwawa*'s signal bridge. The flags and canvas cover for the bag were destroyed in the small fire. Shore leaves were cut short as crew members were ordered back to the ship. Fred Geldmaker, F1C, went on a seven-day leave on December 18 to visit his family in New Jersey for the holidays. On December 21 Fred received a telegram ordering him back to the ship.

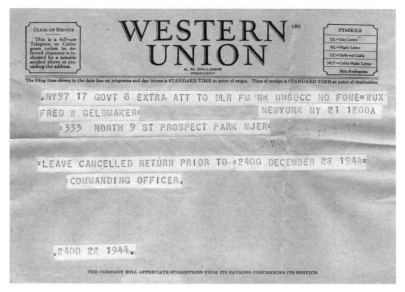

Telegram received by Fred Geldmaker, F1C, canceling his leave.

Preparations for the *Chiwawa*'s departure began on December 22 as the ship was fumigated for pests. All officers and enlisted personnel, except for a small watch group, cleared from the ship until it was deemed safe by Dr. Coughlin and a public health official later that day. On December 23 the crew loaded gasoline aboard and on Christmas Eve the crew loaded Navy Special Fuel Oil and diesel oil.

Chapter 7
Training Operations in the Atlantic

⚓

BY JANUARY 1945 THE *Chiwawa*'s CREW HAD TWO YEARS OF EXPERI-
ence under its belt to pass along to the crews of new ships. Its mission at the time was to train the crews of newly commissioned ships
in the intricacies of refueling ships at sea.

By the time the *Chiwawa* was ready to depart Norfolk, the German attack in France had been stabilized and the trip to Europe
was cancelled. The *Chiwawa* left Norfolk on December 26 bound
for Bermuda, with the newly commissioned USS *Phantom* AM-273 as
escort. While en route, the crew tested the #2 and #4 3-inch guns.
On December 28 the *Chiwawa* parted company from the escort and
arrived in Five Fathom Hole off St. George, Bermuda. Training began
on December 31 with a simulated simultaneous fuel delivery to USS
Manitowoc PF-61 and USS *Diachenko* APD-123. USS *Bivin* APD-536,
USS *Moberly* PF-63, and USS *Albert T. Harris* DE-447 also participated
in the refueling drills. During the training tour in Bermuda some
of the crew took time for personal training, learning new skills or
maintaining skills and keeping their defenses sharp with general
quarters drills and abandon-ship drills. There was also time for re-
laxation. Some of the crew took liberty, touring the area on bicycles

rented for 50 cents a day. Some crew members said they recalled some mischief in the area called The Flats – none revealed what sort of mischief. Cmdr. Goza and Lt. j.g. Leslie Ottman played golf and Les kept the scorecard as a souvenir. On January 26, 1945, Frank Dufour wrote to his sister Marie, "I am hoping we get back to the States soon. I am getting tired of this place. The liberty isn't any good." The crew published an edition of the *Oil Spout* on February 1 after a hiatus beginning the previous June, which brought the crew up to date with all the scuttlebutt from the forecastle to the fantail, including the establishment of a lonely hearts club and New Year's resolutions. The ship's basketball team was reassembled to take on teams from other ships and Navy organizations.

uss *Chiwawa* basketball team 1944–45:

Top Row
Floyd Repsher (left), John Wetzel, David Levins, Art Krieg, Byron Hunter, and Francis Dugan.

Middle Row
Murray Phillips (left) and Richard Catlin.

Bottom Row
Charles Blount (left), James Veacock, Conrad Dion, Murray Hoover, Rene Cournoyer, and James Decker.

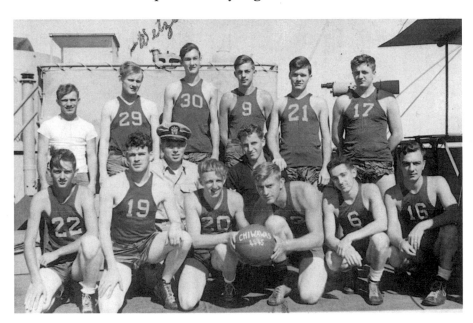

With the end of the war in sight, Cmdr. Goza relaxed some precautionary measures. More information was revealed in the ship's deck log. Until this point in the war, the crew was strictly forbidden from taking pictures while aboard ship or in any military installation. In September of 1944 Ensign Gordon "Gus" Engle reported for duty to the *Chiwawa*. He was an amateur photographer. With the permission of his superiors he started taking pictures aboard ship. Jim Strupp, WT1C, built a darkroom in the fire room to develop the pictures and used the engine room to dry them. Lt. j.g. Jon Bassett recalled that there were pictures lying all over the engine room on

USS *Chiwawa* refuels USS *Springfield* CL-66 on January 13, 1945 near Bermuda.

canvas sheets waiting to dry. The pictures were carefully screened so as not to give away any sensitive information. The pictures were then sold to the crew for 10 cents each. Many of the pictures featured in this book were first developed in the *Chiwawa*'s own darkroom. The series of pictures below were taken on January 13, 1945, as the USS *Springfield* CL-66 completed its shakedown cruise with three practice refueling runs done and one live refueling that delivered 2,214 gallons of Navy Special Fuel Oil.

Over the next 10 days, the *Chiwawa*'s crew engaged in several exercises to train other ships' crews in refueling. Some live runs were mixed in. Many of the ships were destroyer escorts recently converted to high-speed transports (hull designation APD), along with destroyers and patrol craft. One refueled ship of note was USS *Cecil J. Doyle* DE-368. It was the first ship to reach the survivors of USS *Indianapolis* CA-35 after it was torpedoed by the Japanese on July 30, 1945.

In the evening of January 23, while the *Chiwawa* was docked in Great Sound, Bermuda, USS *Sutton* DE-771 struck the *Chiwawa* a glancing blow on her port side between frames 77 and 81. The collision dented the shell plating about nine-and-a-half feet below main deck margin line, leaving a two-inch deep gouge that ran ten inches wide and nine feet long. One longitudinal member was also bent.

At 11:03 P.M. on January 27 the *Chiwawa* left Great Sound, with USS *PCE-847* as escort. The *Chiwawa* spotted the USS *Ira W. Jeffery* DE-63 on January 28. It was part of convoy 18, a non-designated slow-towing convoy consisting of LSTs (Landing Ship Tank), LCI (L) s (Landing Craft Infantry, Large), LCTs (Landing Craft Tank), and two anti-submarine net-laying ships. Some LSTs were being towed and some were under their own power. The convoy left Plymouth, England, bound for Charleston, South Carolina, on December 12, 1944, and was slowed by rough weather and mechanical problems. On December 20 the convoy was 370 miles northeast of San Miguel, Azores Islands, when German submarines attacked. U-870 fired a torpedo, hitting *LST-359* on her port quarter and sinking her, killing three men. USS *Fogg* DE-57 was also torpedoed, ripping apart her stern and killing 15 crewmen. The remaining ships in the convoy limped to Praia Terceira, Azores, and stayed there for repairs and to wait out rough weather. The convoy continued its journey for the

United States on January 9 and again encountered rough seas that slowed its progress.

The unexpected delay depleted USS *Ira Jeffery*'s food and fuel. The men were down to eating hash and rice three times a day. They also had canned bacon rinds picked up as provisions from the British in the Azores, along with a supply of a green vegetable that looked like corn stalks and had the consistency of asparagus stalk – the men never did figure out what it was, said Everett Schrader, SOM1C, who served aboard the *Ira Jeffery*. On January 28 the *Ira Jeffery* crew was very grateful to see the *Chiwawa*, which delivered 1,566 pounds of meat, 1,184 pounds of canned provisions, 96 pounds of lard, 300 pounds of flour and wheat, 60 pounds of butter, 100 pounds of sugar, and 50,000 gallons of Navy Special Fuel Oil.

The identity of the oiler that gave them the desperately needed supplies was a 55-year mystery to the crew of the *Ira Jeffery*, said Schrader, who the author located via the Internet. "You can't believe how good the *Chiwawa* looked the day we saw it and had a feast our first meal after taking on the good stuff from the *Chiwawa*," said Schrader.

After completion of the good deed, the *Chiwawa* returned to Great Sound, arriving at 5:50 P.M. On January 29, the *Chiwawa* departed Great Sound at 8:00 A.M. with USS *Evansville* PF-70 as escort. At 12:55 P.M. the *Chiwawa* sighted Convoy GUS-65 nine miles distant

Joe Kreplick (left) and Ray Kern in Bermuda on February 3, 1945.

and changed course to meet them. At 2:11 P.M. the *Chiwawa* refueled the destroyer escorts of the convoy USS *Edgar Chase* DE-16, USS *John M. Bermingham* DE-530, USS *Andres* DE-45, and USS *Livermore* DD-429. The convoy was delayed by bad weather and consumed more fuel then expected. While approaching the *Chiwawa* USS *Andres* struck it a glancing blow on the starboard quarter, denting the shell plating to a depth of four inches between frames 36 and 40. Frame 38 and one longitudinal member took the main strain. There was no impairment of the operational efficiency of the ship.

In February the crew engaged in more training for refueling at sea. A February 4 exercise with USS *Chevalier* DD-805 was aborted due to rough weather, and both ships returned to port. Frank Dufour wrote to his sister, Marie, on February 5, "You're not kidding there when you said we are getting old. I feel like I am about 50 already." In the morning of February 8 the crew shut down both boilers to make repairs to the exhaust steam line. The emergency diesel generator supplied power and light during the shutdown. The crew completed repairs that afternoon and the ship was ready for duty again.

USS *Chiwawa* Chief Petty Officers February 3, 1945

Top Row
Edward Anderson (left), Alexander Cook, Viateur Roy, John Cunningham, and Frank Ward.

Bottom Row
James Spence (left), William Rhinehardt, Anthony Fusco, Edward Guyer, Albert Campen.

On February 10 the *Chiwawa* left Great Sound, Bermuda, with USS *Herndon* DD-638 and USS *Tillman* DD-641 as escorts, to meet USS *Atlanta* CL-104 for practice and live refueling exercises. Later, the ship's crew engaged in firing practice with port and starboard 40mm guns and stern 5-inch gun shooting at both surface and air balloons. The ship arrived in Five Fathom Hole, Bermuda, on the evening of February 11 and commenced with more refueling training the next day with newly constructed ships USS *Peoria* PF-67, USS *Milledgeville* PF-94, USS *Register* APD-92, USS *Odum* APD-71, and USS *Chevalier* DD-805. With training for the day complete, the *Chiwawa* returned to Great Sound. On February 13 the crew loaded aboard cargo, which included one main propeller shaft, two propellers, two OS2U-3 Kingfisher airplanes, a patrol craft training boat, two expedite boats, and men for transportation to Guantanamo Bay, Cuba. Some of the *Chiwawa*'s men were sent to the States for training and further transfer to different ships. The *Chiwawa* departed on February 17 and arrived in Guantanamo Bay on February 20 to deliver the airplanes and drop off men for new assignments. The ship departed Guantanamo Bay on February 20 and arrived in Aruba on February 22.

Floyd Repsher (left) and Thomas Restani pose with *Chiwawa* deck cargo of an OS2U-3 Kingfisher.

William Davis (left) with Thomas Restani pose with an OS2U-3 Kingfisher.

On February 23 the crew loaded gasoline and Navy Special Fuel Oil. The ship left Aruba for Bermuda unescorted on February 23, arriving at the West Indies Oil Docks February 27. The ship delivered gasoline to the dock. On February 28 the *Chiwawa* moved to Great Sound and moored next to USS *Chemung* AO-30. The crew delivered 1,046,094 gallons of Navy Special Fuel Oil to USS *Chemung* in seven hours. On March 1, while attempting to dock at the Naval Air Station, the ship struck the pier and dented the shell-plating on the starboard side at frame 60 to a depth of about four inches, slightly buckling the frame. The crew delivered Navy Special Fuel Oil to the fuel depot and took on stores, men for transport to Guantanmo Bay for their new assignments, and four airplanes as cargo.

The *Oil Spout* published its last edition on March 1 with comments about a party that the officers enjoyed at the officers' club in Aruba. Francis Rabidou, s1c, was spied measuring the bunks. When asked what he was doing, he responded, "I want to find out how long the boys slept." The publication also included a comment about how glad the crew members were to get orders to go to New York after receiving many changes in orders in the past two months.

With its training duties completed and the defeat of Germany imminent, the crew spent the rest of March transporting fuel and cargo. On March 2 the ship left Bermuda steaming singly, and arrived in Guantanamo Bay on the morning of March 5. The ship dropped off its cargo of men and airplanes and left the same evening for Aruba, steaming singly once again and arriving on March 7. Loaded with Navy Special Fuel Oil and gasoline, the ship set off alone from Aruba at 4:35 A.M. on March 8 en route to Guantanmo Bay. At 3 P.M. the same day the ship was diverted to New York. The rest of the month the ship hauled Navy Special Fuel Oil and gasoline between Aruba and New York, making two round trips steaming singly. The

St. Patrick's Day menu, March 17, 1945.

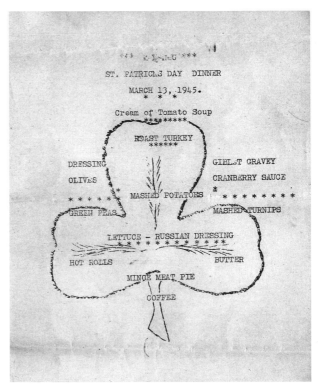

only incident occurred on March 25 just before sunset while traveling from Aruba to New York. An object was sighted in the water. The guns were manned; the forward 3-inch guns and aft 5-inch gun were fired. The object was later identified as a drifting spar.

Frank Dufour wrote to his sister on March 10 that he had a nice suntan and it felt like 120 degrees in the shade.

On St. Patrick's Day the crew ate a special dinner, but corned beef was not on the menu. Instead, the meal featured roast turkey with all the fixings.

Chapter 8
Collision with LSM-III

⚓

THE *Chiwawa* ARRIVED IN NEW YORK JUST BEFORE EASTER WEEK-
end on Thursday, March 29, 1945, with a load of Navy Special Fuel
Oil and gasoline from Aruba. The crew unloaded cargo and men
were transferred to and from the ship. Some crewmen got liberty.
The ship was scheduled to leave New York on Saturday, March 31,
for another trip to Aruba to bring fuel back to New York. The ship,
empty except for its own fuel reserves, left New York harbor unescorted on schedule at 9:01 A.M. The pilot was discharged at 10:04
A.M. as the ship resumed standard speed of 14 knots at 10:06 A.M.
At 10:09 A.M. heavy fog set in with visibility varying from zero to
100 yards. Lt. John Lande, (serving as both the first lieutenant and
cargo officer on the *Chiwawa*) was sent to the bow with extra lookouts. At 10:11 A.M. the *Chiwawa* crew started to sound the fog signal
at one-minute intervals and reduced speed to about 5 knots. The
crew charted a course conforming to the channel and at 10:21 A.M.
increased the ship's speed to 7 knots. At 11:01 A.M. the *Chiwawa*'s
surface-to-ground (S.G.) radar picked up two targets about 25 degrees off the starboard bow – one at 1,300 yards and the other at
1,000 yards – and the crew changed course to avoid contact. At 11:02

A.M. lookouts reported a small vessel approaching about 400 yards away. At 11:03.30 A.M. the *Chiwawa*'s danger signal sounded.

At 11:04 A.M., another ship, *LSM-111* collided with the *Chiwawa* at compass coordinates 40 degrees, 23 minutes north by 73 degrees, 52 minutes west, striking her between frames 50 and 51 and tearing a hole eighteen feet high by ten feet wide. The crew stopped the engines, secured degaussing, and sounded general quarters. At 11:10 A.M. the *Chiwawa* turned back to New York harbor *with LSM-111*. At 11:40 A.M. the fog lifted and *LSM-112* came along the *Chiwawa*'s port side to report the damage to *LSM-111*, as reported in the *Chiwawa* deck log and war diary.

Damage to USS *Chiwawa* as a result of collision with LSM-111 on March 31, 1945.

The ship's collision threw the *Chiwawa*'s Bob Haller, WT1C, out of his bunk. Haller had been sleeping after a return from liberty. Jim Strupp, WT1C, was in the *Chiwawa* fire room at the time of the collision. He said he heard a very loud BANG and the ship rocked. He thought they had been torpedoed. General quarters alarm sounded and he grabbed his Mae West jacket and raced to his 3-inch gun. John Collins, EM3C, sitting in a chair in the steering engine room, was thrown across the room about twelve feet. Bruner Lange, BM2C, said he was standing on the forward port side and grabbed a stanchion to steady himself from the impact of the collision.

Assistant engineering officer Lt. j.g. Jon Bassett was in the engine room until the pilot had left the ship and the bridge had indicated they were done maneuvering the engines. He went to the navigator's quarters visiting with other officers, discussing their destination. Suddenly, he heard seven blasts on the ship's whistle. The room emptied as though it contained a bomb, he recalled, and he headed for the engine room on the run. As he jumped onto the cargo deck from the catwalk, the bow of the other vessel that struck them was just pulling away from the *Chiwawa*'s side and disappeared into the fog. He continued to the engine room and stayed there until the ship returned to the Brooklyn Navy Yard.

Bruner Lange also said as the ship returned to New York after the collision, other ships' crews saluted them – they must have figured that the gaping hole was the work of an enemy torpedo blast.

Frank Dufour wrote to his sister, Marie, on April 1, 1945, "Well kid I bet you are wondering what we are doing in New York. I did tell you in my last letter that I would only be in New York two days. I was right. We pulled out yesterday morning. It was so foggy you couldn't see anything and another ship hit us at mid ship and put a big hole in our side big enough to drive a car into. You don't need to worry we didn't sink. We are in the Brooklyn Navy Yard for a week or so."

A board of inquiry investigated the collision, meeting at the New York Navy Yard at 10 A.M. on April 3, 1945.

The following passage is excerpted from testimony. It is interesting to note that some of the findings of the board are still considered classified in order to protect the men involved in the incident.

The board consisted of Cmdr. Alexander M. Kowalzyk U.S. Navy (senior member); Cmdr. Allen B. Adams Jr., U.S. Navy; Cmdr. Wilbur

C. Hogan, U.S. Coast Guard; and Lt. Elliot J. Friedman, U.S.N.R. as recorder. The first person called to testify was the *Chiwawa*'s captain, Cmdr. John P. Goza, who represented himself.

Goza said he was commanding the ship. Lt. j.g. Martin W. Marquard was the officer of the deck and Lt. j.g. Leslie V. Ottman was the navigator at the time of the incident.

Lt. Ralph D. Cline, the commanding officer of *LSM-111*, testified next. He identified Lt. Arthur F. Lincoln as both the navigator and officer of the deck of *LSM-111* at the time of the collision.

The *Chiwawa*'s Lt. j.g. Martin W. Marquard was next in the hearing. Marquard, gunnery officer and senior officer of the deck, said he took over as officer of the deck of the *Chiwawa* about 10:30 A.M. that morning to relieve a younger officer, Ensign Murray G. Phillips, because of the fog. The ship was proceeding along the channel with the captain in command and himself as officer of the deck. The executive officer and navigator were also on the bridge. The ship had traveled for about 30 minutes when the ship's radar made two radar contacts up ahead that indicated other vessels were in the area and were traveling on the same course as the *Chiwawa*, he stated.

About five minutes before the collision, the radar operator picked up two more contacts coming off of the starboard bow. He sent a messenger into the radar room to check the range and bearing of the contacts. The first range and bearing he got was about 1,500 yards away and about 50 degrees relative on the bow. At that time he could hear the other ship's whistle – its fog signal. The *Chiwawa*'s crew was also sounding a fog signal at that time and he noticed after he got the radar reading that the whistle signals seemed to be getting closer and he went to the starboard side of the bridge in an effort to view the other ship through the fog. He sent the messenger to get another radar reading. The messenger reported that the ships were 900 yards apart and the fog signals were louder, so he knew they were getting very close. That was the last radar range he got before the *LSM-111* appeared out of the fog, he said. The next thing he knew, *LSM-111* appeared out of the fog, bearing approximately 065 degrees relative on the starboard bow. He then put up his binoculars to determine which way he was going. He blew the danger signal on the whistle when he realized the ship was headed on a crash course with the *Chiwawa*.

The executive officer, Lt. Cmdr. George V. Sargent, gave an order for hard right rudder as they tried to swing the ship to avoid contact, but the ship didn't respond quickly enough at the speed they were traveling, Marquard said. As far as he could tell, the *LSM-111* didn't attempt to reduce speed or turn off, but it was hard to tell for sure because it was abaft of his position and at a bad angle, he testified. After the ships collided, general quarters alert was sounded, and the *LSM-111* drifted back into the fog and out of sight. Marquard said Cmdr. Goza, Lt. Cmdr. Sargent (executive officer), Lt. j.g. Ottman (navigator), himself, a quartermaster, helmsman, messenger, radar operator, and other personnel were on the bridge at the time of the accident. There was a regular condition watch (material condition readiness Baker) that included seven men on the bow and 3-inch guns, six men on the flying bridge 40mm gun, 10 men on the five-inch gun aft, two men on the 20mm gun forward, and two men on the after 20mm gun. All men in these positions were instructed to act as lookouts, keeping a sharp eye in their sectors, and to report anything they could see, any whistles they might hear, or anything suspicious. The lookouts were posted when the pilot left the ship. The lookouts did report some fog signals and a few false objects, but were not required to make reports on any time interval. The ship was traveling at five knots from the time he took over as officer of the deck to the time of the collision, though he said the captain was commanding the ship and may have changed the speed without his knowledge. (The deck log noted a speed change at 10:11 A.M. from standard speed, 80 RPM, to one-third speed or 30 RPM, then another speed change at 10:21 A.M. to 40 RPM.)

Marquard said the *Chiwawa* employed surface-to-ground and surface-to-air radar at the time of the collision and that the radar was in use from the time he came on duty. There was a light fog from the time the ship left the harbor, but visibility was not affected much until the ship reached Ambrose Lightship (a stationary lighted ship located at the southern entrance to the harbor), he said. Shortly after that, visibility was reduced to between 100-300 yards. He also said the sea was calm and the wind was from 280 degrees (west-northwest). Marquard said the executive officer gave the command "hard right rudder" for the information of the captain, who was in the charthouse. He said the first radar report he got was after he heard a whistle on the starboard bow. He sent a messenger in to get a bearing and range. The whistle was getting closer, so he asked for another reading and that was the last one he got. He was asked whether the captain was aware of these reports, and he said, "Yes, because the captain was in the radar room when the second report was given." Conrad Dion, RdM2c, was operating the radar and kept records of the radar contacts that morning, he also said.

A crew member in the *Chiwawa*'s 20mm gun nest close to the point of the ship's impact suffered a few scratches in the collision, though that was the only injury that Marquard noted. He said he didn't know if there were any injuries aboard *LSM-111*. He also said the damage-control party on the *Chiwawa* performed well. He said that the only effort initially to ascertain damage to the *LSM-111* was visually from the bridge, but it was difficult to see much because the ship disappeared in the fog. Later the *Chiwawa*'s crew tried to assist via the *LSM-112* about 15 or 20 minutes after the collision as *LSM-112* came alongside to report the damage to *LSM-111*, he said.

He said that Cmdr. Goza was commanding the ship from the time he took over from Ensign Phillips as officer of the deck. The only communication the ships had with each other was the danger signal the *Chiwawa* sounded when the collision was imminent and the fog signals that both ships used. He said he thought the ships were in international waters. The *Chiwawa*'s engines were not stopped at any time when the fog signals appeared to be coming from forward of the beam, Marquard also stated.

During cross-examination from Cmdr. Goza, Marquard said he estimated the speed of *LSM-111* to be 8 knots at the time of the collision.

Lt. Cline, commander of *LSM-111*, cross-examined Lt. j.g. Marquard. He asked who was the legal custodian of the *Chiwawa*'s radar log and if it showed the range and bearing of each contact it made. Marquard said the communications officer was the custodian of the log and that the range and bearing of all contacts were recorded in it. During questioning, Marquard said he received two reports of range and bearing by messenger – the first when the *LSM-111* was about 1,500 yards from the *Chiwawa* at a bearing of about 045 degrees relative to the *Chiwawa*; the second at about 900 yards from the *Chiwawa* and no bearing was recorded because there was no time to get one. He said the executive officer had stepped out onto the starboard wing of the bridge with him and reported the first radar contact with *LSM-111* to the executive officer. After the contact was made, Marquard said the *Chiwawa*'s speed had not changed, but the course had changed to 180, being under hard right rudder.

Marquard testified that he saw Cmdr. Goza through the door of the wheelhouse about 90 seconds before the collision. He said he heard the other ship's fog signals which were at regular intervals from the time he first heard them until the collision. He said he reported the fog signals to the executive officer, who was not commanding the ship at the time.

During questioning by the recorder, Marquard stated that the *Chiwawa* was struck at almost a 90-degree angle and the collision ripped a hole fifteen feet vertically and ten feet diagonally in the *Chiwawa*. Marquard also said he heard a danger signal from *LSM-111* about two minutes before the collision. Cmdr. Goza recross-examined Marquard, who testified that it was not possible to effectively offer assistance to *LSM-111* immediately following the collision.

The board examined Marquard. He testified that considering the speed of the *Chiwawa* at the time of the collision, Marquard said the minimum stopping distance of the ship was about 400 yards, and visibility was about 100 yards at the time. He said the *Chiwawa* was about 10 degrees on the *LSM-111*'s port side at the time that the ship was sighted.

Lt. Cmdr. George V. Sargent, the *Chiwawa*'s executive officer, testified next. Sargent said he began active duty May 12, 1941, and his service aboard the *Chiwawa* began April 1, 1944. He said he had been at sea since June 1941. He testified that he had no specific duty and was on the bridge under his own volition at the time of the collision. He was standing on the starboard wing of the bridge when the ships collided. During the heavy fog conditions he felt he could assist the personnel on the bridge.

The captain was conning the ship at the time of the collision, he said. Asked if he gave any orders to the wheel within fifteen minutes before the collision, Sargent replied, "No, sir. I saw this ship approaching and shouted out to the captain, 'A ship coming in about broad on the starboard bow. Actually a little aft of it, I believe.' That was the first thing I said. Immediately thereafter I said, 'I think we had better come hard right.' That was my opinion based on what was happening."

He also testified, "When the fog set in, which was shortly after we dropped the pilot, we went to one-third speed."

He never gave any orders. Upon his suggestion, "the order was given to the helmsman to come hard right in an attempt to swing our stern away. The annunciators were also put on stop," Sargent reported.

When he saw the ship approaching off of the starboard bow, he called to the bridge the fact that the ship was approaching. A very short interval later he said he thought the ship should come hard right, Sargent testified. He said he thought the captain gave all the orders to the helm. He also testified that the *Chiwawa* sounded fog signals in one-minute intervals beginning about 45 minutes before the collision.

Upon sighting the *LSM-111*, Sargent said, the *Chiwawa* sounded the danger signal – five short blasts – about 20 seconds before the collision. He also testified that there were five surface lookouts stationed on the wings of the flying bridge. He was asked where these men were stationed. He said they were split between the port 40mm gun shield and the starboard 40mm gun shield. There were also regular condition watch lookouts and regular sea watch lookouts, and there were lookouts in the 3-inch gun nest forward, port, and starboard.

Sargent said he heard the signals about fifteen minutes before the accident, and he estimated that *LSM-111* was traveling at a speed of about 12 knots. It was impossible to offer assistance to *LSM-111* following the collision because the explosive condition of the tanks required the immediate attention of the *Chiwawa*'s damage-control personnel, he also noted.

During cross-examination by Lt. Cline, Lt. Cmdr. Sargent said he did not hear any reports from the radar as to the range and bearing of the *LSM-111* prior to the collision, though he said he was not in a position where he would have been able to receive such reports. Sargent said he hadn't heard the officer of the deck send a messenger to get the radar report and that he hadn't heard a messenger give the officer of the deck any information from the radar.

The *Chiwawa's* navigator, Lt. j.g. Leslie V. Ottman, was the next witness called to testify. Ottman said he was navigating the *Chiwawa* at the time of the collision with assistance of the captain. He testified that he kept the commanding officer informed of the navigational position of the ship. He presented the course recorder, the official chart by which the *Chiwawa* was navigated, as well as the rough log and the quartermaster's notebook as evidence.

The *Chiwawa's* chief pharmacist mate, John W. Cunningham, testified that Leroy Thomas Taylor, seaman first class, suffered a scratch on his right cheek along the bone, possibly ½-inch deep, though it did not require stitches. The doctor treated Taylor's wound with a Band-Aid and tincture of Merthiolate, an antiseptic. Cunningham added that no other men were injured in the incident. Taylor's gun nest was about 10 feet from the hole caused by the collision and about 12 feet above the deck, he testified.

Albion Ray Kern, QM3c, the *Chiwawa's* helmsman at the time of the collision, said during testimony that the captain was giving orders at the time of the collision, and that he understood the captain was conning the ship. Kern said he never did see LSM-111 prior to the collision or after, and he estimated that visibility at the time of the crash was zero. "I never saw the LSM-111 at all – it hit aft abeam," he testified.

Prior to the collision, "The captain had given the order full right, and that order came just before the collision. The whole thing seemed like a couple of seconds, I would say," Kern said. The executive officer, Sargent, gave him the same orders –"full right"– at practically the same time the captain gave his orders, Kern said, adding that those were the only orders he received from Sargent. Kern said the captain was going to the starboard wing of the bridge at the time of the collision. When asked if he heard any fog signals given by any ship other than the *Chiwawa* within ten minutes of the collision, Kern said, "I heard a blast – I believe about the time we hit, maybe a little before." Asked if the blast came from the LSM-111, Kern said he wasn't sure, though the blast did sound like it emanated from the direction in which the LSM-111 appeared on the starboard side. Kern also said he couldn't determine whether the blast came from forward of the beam.

During questioning by Lt. Cline, Kern said he believed the *Chiwawa* was still swinging left when the ships collided.

Conrad Dion, RdM2c, the *Chiwawa*'s radar man at the time of the collision, testified next. He produced a radar record of the ranges and bearings of objects taken on the morning of the collision as evidence. Dion testified that he got some ranges and bearings of objects on the radar prior to the collision with the *LSM-111*. His first range and bearing relating to the *LSM-111* was 1,100 yards, bearing 190 degrees, Dion said. The first contact was at 11 A.M., just as he had finished tuning up his gear. Dion reported that he provided information on ranges and bearings to the captain.

During questioning by Goza, Dion stated that the radar showed "two ships close together" with the range of the farthest target at 1,300 yards and the bearing of the second target almost astern of the *LSM-111*. Asked if there were any other targets, Dion replied, "Yes, there were quite a few targets all around us." Dion also stated that he was not able to record the range and bearing of all the targets on the radar screen. The plotting officer (Ensign Elliott Royce) was being rushed – he was working with my range and bearing on this ship."

In cross-examination by Lt. Cline, Dion said the radar was George (surface radar) and it had a PPI screen. (A PPI screen, or Plan Position Indicator, is a cathode ray tube much like a television screen. It is a polar display of the surrounding area, with one ship represented by the origin of the sweep, normally located in the center of the scope. The PPI provided a map-like picture of the area covered by the radar beam.) Dion said the log showed one range and bearing taken on the *LSM-111*.

During questioning by Goza, Dion said it was difficult to maintain his watch and record the bearings because there were many targets to take care of at that moment.

Dion also testified that the radar antenna was rotating continuously until he picked up the *LSM-111* and then he continued to rotate it by hand. Dion said the radar gear was running fair, but he couldn't get maximum pip on it.

The board then examined Dion. He told the board that he gave radar reports to the plotting officer next to him and that officer gave it to the messenger, who then would give it to the officer of the deck. The reports were also given by voice tube, Dion also said.

After the examination of Dion, the investigation adjourned for the day at 5 P.M. It resumed at 9 A.M. on April 4.

The recorder called Lt. Cmdr. Vernon Ralph Hayes of the New York Navy Yard to testify. Hayes submitted a job order listing the required repairs to the *Chiwawa* as evidence. The job order listed the cost of the repairs to the *Chiwawa* as $18,345, and the order estimated that the repair work, scheduled to start April 5, would take ten days.

Lt. John Lande, who served as a lookout on the *Chiwawa*'s forecastle at the time of the collision, testified next. Lande, whose duties included first lieutenant, cargo officer, deck court officer, and damage control officer, said the crew started pumping out the aft end of the ship following the collision to get the ruptured plate above the water level. He said the draft increased as a result of the collision an inch or two. The ship had no list before, but it had a six-degree list to port after the collision, he reported. The *Chiwawa* had no cargo – just water ballast – at the time of the collision, and the only oil the ship carried was bunker oil for fuel, Lande also testified. No compartments were flooded as a result of the collision, but the crew flooded one or two tanks to get her back on an even keel, he said.

He said the ship's shell plate was ruptured in the collision, and there was likely some damage to the degaussing cable, too. The shell plating outside number seven wing tank was ruptured at frame 51, he added. The damage was eighteen feet high by eight feet wide, extending from the main deck to the waterline, and lengthwise between frames 50 and 51. He said the damaged plate extended below the waterline about a foot or two before the crew began to shift weights.

The material condition of readiness was Baker aboard the *Chiwawa* before the collision, and general quarters was sounded immediately after the collision. The ship took about an eight-degree list to port, as the rupture caused water to flood out of number seven starboard wing tank, Lande said. The crew immediately opened up the suction valves of the number seven port wing tank and number six starboard wing tank, and also opened the suction valves of number four main and number four starboard wing tank, causing flooding into the empty number six starboard wing tank and number four starboard wing tank, which was at the waterline level. Fire hoses were stretched out on deck as a precautionary measure, he said. There was no failure of equipment aboard the *Chiwawa*, he said, and the repair party worked very quickly and took the list off the ship so the hole was above the waterline. No fires broke out after the collision, though Lande said there was some danger of fire or explosion because the ruptured shell plate was about three feet away from number eight wing tank, which was an empty tank but contained some fumes.

Lande testified that prior to the collision he spotted the *LSM-111* about 200-300 yards from the *Chiwawa* and reported it to the bridge. The visibility was poor, he also testified, and he could only see about 300 yards. He testified that he heard fog signals from the *LSM-111* just prior to the time he reported the ship to the bridge. The fog signal came in the form of one prolonged blast coming from ahead, and he said that from the time he was on the forecastle he heard about six or eight fog signals, which he assumed were from ships going in the same direction as the *Chiwawa*. In the five minutes prior to the collision, he said he heard one fog signal from the *LSM-111* just before the collision.

Lande said there was a telephone in the gun nest, but he chose to shout and wave his hand to indicate the direction of the approaching ship.

Lande said he hadn't heard any other sound signals from the direction in which the *LSM* eventually appeared – the sound signals that he heard gave him the impression that they came from ahead and they didn't appear to get any closer. He said he figured the sounds came from ships traveling in the same direction. During the time he acted as a lookout, Lande said he heard several fog signals from forward of the beam.

Lande testified that he didn't recall reporting any fog signals to the bridge – he reported once that he could see a ship, but it didn't turn out to be anything. He was also told to look for a buoy and never saw it. He testified that he never reported any of the fog signals because he assumed they heard them on the bridge.

Lt. j.g. Lester Gawlocki, the *Chiwawa*'s chief engineering officer, testified next. He submitted the *Chiwawa*'s bell book and engineering log for March 31, 1945, as evidence. The *Chiwawa* had one shaft, he testified, and he couldn't recall the ship's standard speed at the time of the collision. Standard speed varied, Gawlocki said. He was under the impression it may have been 80 turns, but he couldn't make a definite statement. In reference to the bell book, he said an entry at 8:52 A.M. of one-third speed at 40 revolutions per minute (RPM) represented an engine speed of 7.8 knots, and an entry at 9:06 A.M. of two-thirds speed at 60 (RPM) represented a speed of 11.8 knots. He said he didn't know the speed of the ship in terms of RPM at 9:11 A.M. because there was no entry for standard speed in the RPM column. He said the *Chiwawa* was making 7.8 knots by engine at the time of the collision, though he didn't know how fast the ship was traveling through the water. Immediately after the collision, Gawlocki said the *Chiwawa* was stopped – the screw was stopped for six minutes. When the screw was started up again, the ship traveled at one-third speed at 30 RPM, he said.

At the time of the collision, Gawlocki said, he was in the amidships deckhouse and was not on duty.

Lt. j.g. Arthur F. Lincoln the *LSM-111*'s executive officer, testified next and submitted the ship's navigational chart, the rough deck log, and the quartermaster's notebook as evidence. In the collision, both of the *LSM-111*'s bow doors were smashed beyond repair, and the plating on the starboard side directly aft of the starboard bow door was damaged and had to be removed. The ship was damaged back about eighteen inches from the aft end of the bow doors and had numerous holes along the plating directly behind the bow doors. There was a small hole in the forward void space below the bow doors. Both doors required removal and replacement, he said. The ship's draft forward was approximately four feet and the draft aft was approximately six feet prior to the collision, and there was no change after the collision. The *LSM-111* wasn't carrying any load, he said, and the ship carried ordinary gear when cruising and no excess cargo. No compartments aboard the ship were flooded as a result of the collision. The ship was at material condition of readiness Baker prior to the collision. Lincoln said he was serving as officer of the deck and navigator on the 8 A.M. to noon watch. After the collision, Lincoln said the crew installed a cofferdam (provided on LSMs) across the inner part of the bow to prevent any water from coming in on the deck. Lincoln said damage control had succeeded in controlling the situation and the cofferdam was not needed.

The captain was conning the ship at the time of the collision, he said. The captain took over when the radar bearing showed the other vessel was coming in the danger area, about five or six minutes before the collision, Lincoln said. At 10:57 A.M. the LSM-111 changed course. About the same time the ship started receiving radar reports on the *Chiwawa* and they were steering almost a reciprocal course of the LSM's course, Lincoln testified. The LSM-112 was about 500 yards directly behind the LSM-111, he reported. About two minutes before the collision the *Chiwawa*'s relative bearings between the LSM-111 and the *Chiwawa* changed rapidly, indicating the *Chiwawa* had made a change in course to port, and about one minute before the accident the LSM's crew could sight the ship's wake through the fog, Lincoln said. The *Chiwawa* appeared to be cutting across the LSM's bow from the LSM's port to its starboard, he added, and the LSM's captain ordered the engines all back emergency full and hard left rudder. The engines started backing when the LSM-111 struck the *Chiwawa* on its starboard quarter, Lincoln reported. "We struck it at about a 70-degree angle and since we were backing, the two ships parted almost immediately. We laid to for approximately fifteen minutes at the scene of the accident then proceeded on into New York," he said. General quarters alert was not sounded, he said – the ship was blowing danger signals as soon as the accident occurred to warn LSM-112.

Asked about the operational orders for LSM-111 on March 31, 1945, Lincoln said that the ship was proceeding from Norfolk, Virginia, to New York City, New York to pick up cargo. The LSM-112, the senior vessel, was accompanying the LSM-111. Lincoln said he was on the bridge at the time of the collision, along with the captain, quartermaster second class Hunt, and Jones, seaman first class serving as the lookout. Lincoln said the ship had sounded one long blast every minute since 8 A.M. on March 31 and continued to sound signals during his watch. Lincoln said the LSM-111 was proceeding on international rules concerning the fog. The *Chiwawa*'s fog signals, he said, were not very distinct and seemed rather irregular prior to the collision, he testified.

"There were several other ships in our vicinity, including *LSM-112*, and the radar reported several other ships ahead of us so it is really rather hard to determine which ones we did hear from the *Chiwawa*, but we did hear fog signals that we thought came from the ship bearing down on us," he reported. He said the fog signals seemed to come from the direction of the port bow. Lincoln said the engines were not stopped when the signals were heard. He said visibility was about 500-600 yards at the time of the collision.

Lincoln also said that he served as officer of the deck until a short time before the collision, giving all orders from the conn. The captain took over the conn when danger seemed imminent, he said, and the captain gave the order of hard left rudder and all engines back emergency full just before the collision. Lincoln said the communications were shouted from a distance of about 75-100 feet. The lookout on the conn reported seeing the *Chiwawa* just prior to the collision, but by that time the officers had already seen the ship, too, Lincoln said. The *Chiwawa* was about 500 yards away when it was sighted, he said. The *LSM-111* was equipped with S08 radar equipment, Lincoln also said, and he read from the ship's radar-bearing book about the first radar sighting of the *Chiwawa*. "The radar reported the first report at about 2,500 yards, bearing of 348 relative from us, and the bearings continued on 348 relative for about two minutes. Then they suddenly started to change from 348 up to approximately 354. At that time they were too close to show on our scope because we had already sighted them by then," Lincoln said.

The sea was calm and the wind was very light at the time of the collision, he said. Lincoln testified that the collision took place at approximately 11:04 A.M. No personnel aboard *LSM-111* were injured in the collision, he said, save for a few scratches. No whistle signals were exchanged with the *Chiwawa* from the time of the sighting of the *Chiwawa* until the collision, Lincoln also testified. *LSM-111* sounded prescribed fog signals prior to the collision and the danger signals after the collision, he said. The *LSM-111* was steering a course of 011 true prior to coming to 359 at 10:57 A.M., Lincoln said. Asked how fast the *LSM-111* was traveling prior to the time of the collision, Lincoln replied, "I hesitate to answer that question." The engines were ordered emergency full back as soon as the *Chiwawa* was sighted at a distance of about 500-600 yards, he testified, and he said the ship had been traveling at about 12 knots since it left Norfolk. Lt. Carroll, the senior officer present on the LSM-112, had determined this speed of 12 knots, Lincoln reported.

Goza in cross-examination asked whether Lincoln considered the LSM-111's speed to be compliant with Article 16 of the International Rules regarding moderate speed in a fog. Lincoln replied that LSMs are supposed to be able to gather sternway in 37 seconds from standard speed ahead. Based on an estimated visibility of 500 to 600 yards, the LSM should have been able to stop in the distance of this visibility. Lincoln said that the entrance to the harbor was considered to be a congested area, and the ship had its radar operating and "had a pretty good idea of where everything was around us." Lincoln also testified that he knew, as navigating officer, that LSM-111 was approaching the swept channel.

Lincoln said the senior officer of LSM-112 gave the orders to LSM-111. The ship traveled on the prescribed small craft course – Marci Baker – he said. LSM-111 and LSM-112 both reported targets ahead of them in radar readings, he said, though no officer in command of LSM-112 gave the LSM-111 any orders for change in course or speed in response to this radar report. Lincoln said he estimated visibility at about 500-600 yards because the LSM-111's radar reported that LSM-112 was about 500 yards astern, and the ship was visible at that distance. The ship had been using this method to estimate visibility for about thirty minutes, Lincoln testified, and the visibility appeared to remain constant during this time. LSM-111's course changed slightly after the captain ordered the hard left rudder, Lincoln said, but there was no prior order to change course. By the time the captain ordered hard left rudder, it was too late to have much effect on the ship's course, Lincoln said.

Lincoln said he estimated that it took about a minute for the ships to collide after the *Chiwawa* was first sighted.

Lincoln testified that the captain had been informed that a fog had set in. The captain was not present at the conning station during the entire watch, Lincoln said, but was there about thirty minutes prior to the collision, Lincoln testified. The captain took over the conn "when the situation was becoming dangerous," Lincoln said. The LSM-111 made first radar contact with the *Chiwawa* about seven to eight minutes prior to the collision, Lincoln said, and the captain was notified of this contact. The ship did not begin a radar plot because it did not carry radar plots, Lincoln also reported. Instead, the crew reported radar bearings in a bearing book. When the two LSMs left Norfolk, the senior officer on *LSM-112* told *LSM-111* to take the lead, and he established his own distance aft of it, Lincoln testified. There was no set distance or formation as far as he knew, Lincoln said. The radar bearings on the *Chiwawa* didn't remain steady for a very long period of time, Lincoln also said, adding that he did not consider at first that the course and speed at which he was proceeding might possibly result in a collision or involve the ship in a dangerous situation. Lincoln said he did not report the radar contact that eventually proved to be the *Chiwawa* when the radar operator reported that he had contact of ships ahead. Lincoln did not request that the commanding officer of *LSM-112* alter course or speed as a result of the contact, he also said. When the *LSM-111* made the first radar contact with the *Chiwawa* at 10:57 A.M., the captain took over the conn, Lincoln reported.

This was about seven minutes before the collision, he said. The commanding officer of *LSM-112* used the loud hailer to notify the *LSM-111* that the ships were going to change course at 10:57 A.M., Lincoln said. The two commanding officers of the *LSM-111* and *LSM-112* directed the change that was going to be made at 10:57 A.M., he said. "My commanding officer consulted his chart and they agreed between themselves that the course was to be changed at 10:57 A.M., according to the original base course we had plotted in Norfolk." He said his own commanding officer did not make any recommendations relative to course to be steered, based upon the close proximity of the radar target, which later proved to be the *Chiwawa*. The radar contact had not been made prior to the change of course at 10:57 A.M., he also said. The captain did not make any further recommendation to the commanding officer of *LSM-112* taking into consideration the radar contact. The commanding officer of *LSM-111* did not recommend a change in speed after radar contact was made at about 10:57 A.M., Lincoln said. The senior officer present prescribed the speed they were to use in traveling to New York City, he testified. Lincoln said he didn't know whether the commanding officer of *LSM-111* recommended a reduction in speed when visibility was reduced.

He also testified that he did not advise his commanding officer at any time that his ship was heading into danger.

Goza recross-examined Lincoln. During questioning, Lincoln said that range and bearing of the radar contract made at 10:57 A.M. was 2,500 yards, 348 degrees relative.

The board asked Lincoln to produce the *LSM-111*'s radar log, and questioned Lincoln about an entry at 10:48 A.M. and the notation of 4.5. The notation signified miles, he said, and he didn't know whether that radar contact was the *Chiwawa*. He also said he didn't think that another radar entry, of two miles bearing 358 at 10:56 A.M., was the *Chiwawa*. The book stated that for the entry at 10:56 A.M., the type of target was a ship, and Lincoln said the radar contact "could have been" the *Chiwawa*. "We would have had to make a course change to be that (ship)." In earlier testimony, Lincoln had referred to a course change made at 10:57 A.M., and he said the course change might mean that the early radar contact was the *Chiwawa*. "That is right. That could be them," he said.

Lt. Cmdr. Clarence Leroy Clark, assistant planner and estimator for hull at Bayonne Annex Navy Yard in New York, testified next. Clark said the damage and repairs to *LSM-111* would cost about $8,946.

George F. Regan, RdM3c, on duty as radar operator aboard *LSM-111* at the time of the collision, said there was a target just inside the 5-mile range marker. He noted it in a log entry at 10:48 A.M. Regan said he believed that he reported this contact to the officer of the deck on the conn. "And then I started to report a target which appeared at the two marker position at approximately 10:56." He spotted an object at a range of 2,500 yards at about 10:58 A.M. and at 1,800 yards at 10:59 A.M. He said he reported this 10:59 A.M. bearing to the conning tower, but not to any particular officer. The next bearing, at 11:01 A.M., showed an object at 700 yards that appeared to be a ship. At about 11:02 A.M., Regan said the same object was at 500 yards and 354 degrees relative to *LSM-111*. He said he reported this to Lincoln, who he believed was the officer in charge of the conn, via voice tube. His report was acknowledged. After the 11:02 A.M. bearing, Regan reported that the object appeared in the center of the radar screen and was not visible. Soon after the ships collided, the object appeared again, but it was pulling away. The range was increasing from *LSM-111*, he added.

John B. Hunt, Jr., QM2c, testified next. Hunt, who was standing in for the quartermaster striker assigned to the watch, testified that the visibility was about 300-500 yards at the time of the collision. The *Chiwawa* sounded fog signals prior to the collision, he said, though they "were not very distinct or very regular." Hunt said he heard a fog signal about two or three minutes before the collision, though he wasn't sure whether the fog signal he heard came from the direction in which the *Chiwawa* eventually appeared. After Hunt's testimony, the board adjourned for the day.

The board met again at 9 A.M. on April 5, 1945.

Woodrow Bennett, GM2c, helmsman aboard the *LSM-111* the time of the collision, said he saw the *Chiwawa* just before the collision. Bennett testified that *LSM-111* was swinging left at the time of the collision in response to the captain's orders. The whistle cord was on his left side, overhead about two feet, Bennett reported, and Mears, S1c, was manning the whistle cord and making a signal once each minute. Prior to the collision, Bennett said he was watching the annunciator and compass, and he didn't see the *Chiwawa* until the ships were very close to striking.

Lt. Cline, who requested that he be called as a witness on his own behalf, testified that shortly after *LSM-111* changed course he received a radar report of a target, apparently a ship, at a distance of 1.25 miles. Cline said that "it would be impossible" for this to be the same target that was recorded prior to changing course, because he was on a heading of 011 degrees and the reported target was on bearing 358. That would put it almost dead ahead of him, Cline said, and by swinging left – which he did – that would place the object on his starboard bow, where before it was on the port bow.

Cline said that based on what the radar man told him, there were other reports that appeared to track the same object that was reported at 10:58 A.M. Cline said he heard signals ahead but couldn't pinpoint their location. He had been hearing signals from 10:30 A.M. on as the *LSM-111* passed other ships. From the next radar report, Cline testified that he figured the object on radar would cross in front on the *LSM-111*'s bow and pass safely astern of the ship. Cline also said he didn't stop because *LSM-112* was astern of him and it would place his ship in danger of being rammed by *LSM-112*. *LSM-112* was traveling at a speed of about 12 knots and followed directly astern of him, Cline said. The LSMs were in contact with SCR, or short wave radio, Cline testified, and he had initiated the communications. The *Chiwawa* was about 350-400 yards away when he first saw it, Cline said. He considered LSM-111 to be the privileged vessel because the *Chiwawa* was coming on his port bow.

The recorder asked whether 12 knots was considered a safe speed for the conditions. Cline answered "Yes and no," adding that visibility ranged from 1,000 yards at one place to 200-300 yards in another. Visibility within five minutes of the collision was about 400 yards, he testified. The low-visibility conditions "would come and go. There were breaks in the fog," Cline said. The recorder asked, "Then I repeat my original question: Did you consider your speed that you were making under the conditions that existed, the speed of 12 knots, a safe speed?" Cline said, "No."

Cline said he didn't change the ship's speed because he received a radar contact from the ship ahead and he had to take into account the LSM-112 astern of him. After receiving the contact, he changed course, and as the privileged vessel, maintained speed and course, he said. The recorder asked whether he attempted to contact LSM-112 after he came to the opinion that the speed of 12 knots was not a safe speed. Cline said he had not, because he had just been in contact with the LSM-112 moments before. In that conversation with the LSM-112, Cline reportedly asked, "Do you have those ships ahead on your radar screen?" to which the reply was, "Yes, are they clear to you?" The recorder asked whether that was the entire conversation, and Cline said he remained on SCR – remained on orders. Cline said he did not specifically raise the question of whether the ships were proceeding at an unsafe speed, though he said he thought this issue was addressed when he asked whether the LSM-112 saw the target ahead.

The recorder asked whether Cline felt that he should have exercised any control over the speed of LSM-111 when the speed of the ship became unsafe, and Cline said, "Not right at that time, no, sir." Cline said that during the LSM-111's final shakedown in Galveston, Texas, he was at the conn of the ship in a crash stop landing in front of an observation party on the final inspection board. In that case, the ship built up speed to standard ahead which is 11 knots or 11.4 for their tonnage at the time, and it took 37 seconds from the time the crash stop landing was recorded until the ship had sternway on. In the collision with the *Chiwawa*, the LSM-111 didn't have full speed up, but it was moving astern. Cline said he believed that in 37 seconds the ship could travel 240-250 yards during the crash stop landing. Cline said LSM-111 slowed down but did not stop when whistle signals were heard ahead from 10:30 A.M. on. Based on his understanding of "rules of the road" when fog signals are heard ahead, Cline said that a vessel shall stop and not proceed until it is determined where the fog signals are coming from. He also said that it seemed clear that the fog signals were coming from forward of the beam, and based on these "rules of the road," ships must be able to stop within half the distance of visibility when traveling in fog.

Cline testified that he knew he was entering a swept channel, and he took into consideration the possibility that deep draft vessels are limited to that swept channel. He also said he didn't figure that the *Chiwawa* was in the channel – it was slightly out of the channel, to the west of the channel. Upon exiting Chesapeake Bay the LSM-112 directed the LSM-111 to take the lead, traveling directly in front of LSM-112. Cline said there was no specific or set distance apart that was prescribed for LSM-111 and LSM-112. LSM-111 was designated as guide ship by blinker, he said. The speed for the ships was set at a conference the night before the ships left port. Cline said he asked Lt. Carroll what speed to make and Carroll said full speed. Cline said he then asked whether he understood that to mean 12 knots, and Lt. Carroll reportedly told him, "Yes, sir." During the voyage Cline said that both ships navigated with the buoys and traveled up the smaller craft route for most of the trip on the way to New York. With one exception, all of the changes in formation, course, and speed were done independently by each ship, he told the board. Cline said he was once ordered through SCR and next by loud hailer from LSM-112 about a change in course. The change in course at 10:57 A.M. was not made by executive method, Cline said. Lt. Carroll reportedly came along his port side approximately 400 yards shortly before that and said by loud hailer that he thought they better change to 359. Cline said he asked, "All right, at what time?" Lt. Carroll set the time and said, "I will follow astern of you." Cline said that he did not believe that this positioning would be considered maneuvering in close formation in the naval sense of the term.

The board asked whether Cline felt that he "properly could break formation to maneuver as circumstances dictated regardless of the signaled course and speed in effect at the time" if the safety of his own vessel was at stake. Cline answered, "I think that is true at any time, Commander." Cline said he believed that the other vessel was the burdened vessel because it was coming to the LSM's port bow, and according to the rules that made him the privileged vessel.

He testified that he assumed he had the right of way just from the radar contact, although he acknowledged that this contact did not prove right of way. When he sighted the *Chiwawa*, Cline said danger of a collision was imminent. It was the responsibility of both ships to sound the danger signal and to try to get clear of each other when the danger of collision existed, he said. Neither vessel was burdened when danger of collision existed, and he changed course upon sighting the *Chiwawa*, he also said. Cline said that under General Prudential Rules, both vessels are required to take whatever action is possible to avoid collision. "Yes, sir; that is what I done, commander," he testified. Cline said during testimony that it appeared as though the *Chiwawa* was no more burdened than his vessel. He said, too, that the exchange of radar report information between the LSM-111 and LSM-112 might have been more appropriately communicated by SCR "or other appropriate means."

The *Chiwawa*'s Lt. Cmdr. George V. Sargent testified next. He said he saw the officer of the deck sounding the danger signal when the LSM-111 was sighted. Immediately thereafter the officer of the deck shouted down to the 20mm gun nest, starboard side amidships, to clear that nest of personnel who were stationed there on watch. The nest was about ten feet forward of the point of actual collision. He noticed that the men in the nest seemed to be frozen. Without a doubt, he thought the officer of the deck did, by his actions, assist in clearing that nest faster than if it had been left up to the men themselves. He said he believed it was exemplary because there might have been injuries if the LSM-111 had struck that nest in the collision. Sargent also said he did not believe the officer of the deck was able to do too much more during that short interval.

The board took a recess and reconvened. No more witnesses were called. The board reported the following finding of facts:

1. The USS *Chiwawa* (AO-68), commanded by Cmdr. John P. Goza and USS *LSM-111*, commanded by Lt. Ralph D. Cline collided in approximate position Latitude 40 degrees, 22 minutes, 0 seconds N, Longitude 73 degrees, 50 minutes, 30 seconds W, bearing 105 degrees true, distance 6.7 miles from Navesink Lighthouse as determined by the board from course recordings, best available information as to speeds and computation of currents, at about 1104 Zone (plus) 4 time, March 31, 1945. This position is about 400 yards west of the New York Swept channel.

2. The USS *Chiwawa* was proceeding on various courses averaging about 160 degrees true at 40 RPM (7.2 knots) from New York seaward via New York swept channel. At 11:00 A.M. radar bearings were obtained on an object bearing 190 degrees true at 1,100 yards and simultaneously another object bearing 196 degrees true distance 1,300 yards. At 11:01 A.M. the order was issued to change course to 150 degrees true. At 11:02 A.M. the order was changed to come left to 130 degrees true. Before the course change was completed, and about 11:03 A.M., the USS *LSM-111* was sighted about 20 degrees forward of the starboard beam. At this instant hard right rudder was ordered but by reason of the momentum of the ship she continued to swing left until 110, at which time the ship's head was approximately 130 degrees true and at which time the collision with *LSM-111* occurred.

3. The *LSM-111* and *LSM-112*, the latter being the senior ship, were proceeding in company from Norfolk, Virginia, to New York City, New York, via Marci Baker route. At about 10:48 A.M. while on course 011 degrees true, at full speed (12 plus knots) the USS *LSM-111* obtained radar contact with an object bearing 348 degrees relative, distance 4.5 miles. At 10:56 A.M. according to the radar log, bearing was obtained on a target on bearing 358 degrees relative distance 2 miles. At about 10:57 A.M. the course was altered to 359 degrees true, speed remaining full. At 10:58 A.M. radar contact was obtained with an object bearing 348 degrees relative, distance 2,500 yards. At 10:59 A.M. this bearing was steady and range had decreased to 1,800 yards. By about 11:01 A.M. the bearing had changed to 352 relative and the range

had decreased to 700 yards. At about 11:02 A.M. the bearing had changed to 354 degrees relative and range decreased to 500 yards. Shortly thereafter, at about 11:03 A.M., the USS *Chiwawa* was sighted bearing about 350 degrees relative, distance about 300 yards. The engines were ordered to back emergency full and hard left rudder was ordered. Before these measures could take effect, the USS *LSM-111* struck the USS *Chiwawa* on the starboard side between frames 53 and 55.

4. The commanding officer of the USS *Chiwawa* was on the bridge and in the wheelhouse and had the conn since 10:07 A.M., at which time the ship had stopped abeam of Gedney Buoy to drop the pilot.

5. The commanding officer of the USS *LSM-111* had been on the conning station all morning but did not assume the conn until shortly before the collision occurred.

6. Lt. j.g. Martin W. Marquard was the officer of the deck of the USS *Chiwawa*, having assumed these duties at about 10:30 A.M.

7. Lt. j.g. Arthur F. Lincoln was officer of the deck of USS *LSM-111*, having assumed these duties about 8 A.M.

8. At the time of the collision the weather was foggy, visibility about 300 yards, the wind was slight and the tidal current was flowing toward 280 degrees true with a velocity of approximately 0.2 knot.

9. Both ship's fog lookouts were stationed in accordance with standard instructions.

10. Both vessels were sounding fog signals in accordance with the International Rules for Preventing Collisions.

11. Upon mutually sighting each other, neither vessel sounded the signals for passing as prescribed by Article 28 of the International Rules for Preventing Collisions, although both vessels

sounded the danger signal prescribed by Article 18 of the Inland Rules for Preventing Collisions.

12. Upon hearing a fog signal forward of the beam, neither vessel stopped engines as prescribed by Article 16 of the International Rules for Preventing Collisions.

13. Both vessels were equipped with radar which was manned and operating satisfactorily.

14. USS *LSM-111* was not maintaining a continuous radar plot.

15. In both vessels all orders were executed promptly upon receipt.

16. No material defects contributed to this collision.

17. Prior to the collision both vessels were in material condition Baker.

18. Immediately upon sighting USS *LSM-111*, USS *Chiwawa* went to general quarters and instituted measures for controlling damage incident to collision.

19. USS *LSM-111* did not go to general quarters or sound collision quarters, but the repair parties immediately after the collision instituted damage-control measures.

20. *LSM-111* had a draft of 4 feet forward and 6 feet aft immediately prior to and following the collision.

21. USS *Chiwawa* had a draft of 18 feet 6 inches forward and 27 feet aft immediately prior to the collision. Immediately following the collision USS *Chiwawa* took a list to port of 6 to 8 degrees and her mean draft was reduced approximately 2 inches. This list and reduction of draft were caused by the escape of water ballast from number seven wing tank through the hole caused by the collision. This tank had been completely filled and contained

a considerable volume of water above the waterline. The list was corrected by the damage control party within five minutes.

22. Neither vessel rendered assistance to the other, but the USS *LSM-112*, which was present at the time, came close aboard the USS *Chiwawa* at about 11:40 A.M. and advised the commanding officer that the *LSM-111* was proceeding to New York. Neither vessel required assistance.

23. The damage sustained by the USS *Chiwawa* is described as follows:

    (a) A hole was torn in the shell plating 10 feet wide in the fore and aft direction and 18 feet in length extending from the main deck to 2 feet below the waterline, including the portion of deck stringer plate about 14 feet long by 15 inches wide between framcs 53 and 55 starboard.

    (b) Structural framing in the above area was also damaged.

    (c) The degaussing cable between frames 53 and 55 was damaged to such an extent as to require replacement of the section between existing connection boxes at frame 41 starboard side of engine room and at frame 62 starboard side of workshop, upper level.

24. The cost of necessary repairs to the USS *Chiwawa* is estimated to be $18,345.

25. The time necessary to effect repairs to the USS *Chiwawa* is estimated to be 10 days.

26. The damage sustained by the USS *LSM-111* is described in detail as follows:

    (a) Bow doors: Damage to port and starboard bow doors beyond economical repair. Hinge pads, dogs, and door fittings sprung. Door flap hoist cables parted.

(b) Port structure: Second superstructure deck between frames 4 and 5 from shell plating to inboard bulkhead buckled. Sloping watertight bulkhead, frame 4 fractured at top hinge pad. Hydraulic ram guard above second superstructure deck between frames 4 and 5 torn away from ship.

(c) Starboard structure: Shell plating inboard breast-hooks, sloping watertight bulkhead frame 4, hydraulic ram guard and second superstructure deck crumpled and fractured between frames 4 and 5 from about the 11-foot waterline.

(d) Hydraulic Units: Hydraulic cylinders, ram and foundation, port and starboard, beyond economical repair.

(e) Fore peak: Forward end of starboard end starboard side between 2 feet and 3 feet off centerline at shell and main deck indented about 2 inches.

(f) Bow ramp: Starboard outboard stringer flange of bow ramp bent.

27. The cost of necessary repairs to the USS *LSM-111* is estimated to be $8,946, exclusive of bow doors and hydraulic operating gear to be furnished by the Bureau of Ships, the cost of which is not available.

28. The time necessary to effect repairs to the *LSM-111* is estimated to be 10 days.

29. No injuries sufficient to warrant medical treatment to personnel in the *LSM-111* resulted from the collision. Leroy Thomas Taylor Jr. S1C, member of USS *Chiwawa* crew, sustained minor injuries but not to the extent of being admitted to the sick list.

The following is the opinion of the board of inquiry:

1. The major responsibility for the collision between the USS *LSM-111* and USS *Chiwawa* rests with the commanding officer of the USS *LSM-111*, Lt. Ralph D. Cline, in that:

    (a) In view of the normally congested area in which his vessel was operating, and the very reduced visibility caused by fog, his vessel was maintaining full speed, 12 knots, a speed far in excess of the speed permissible under Article 16 of the International Rules for Preventing Collisions.

    (b) He failed to cause the engines of the USS *LSM-111* to be stopped and to navigate with caution when hearing a fog signal forward of the beam as required under Article 16 of the International Rules for Preventing Collisions.

    (c) He failed to cause a continuous radar plot to be maintained.

    (d) Having a radar contact on a steady bearing with diminishing range, he failed to take any action to avoid a collision as ordinary prudence, good judgment, and proper seamanship would dictate.

2. A portion of the responsibility between the USS *LSM-111* and the USS *Chiwawa* also rests with the commanding officer of the USS *Chiwawa*, Cmdr. John P. Goza, in that:

    (a) In view of a normally congested area in which his vessel was operating, and the very reduced visibility caused by fog, his vessel was maintaining one-third speed, seven knots, a speed slightly in excess of the speed permissible under Article 16 of the International Rules for Preventing Collisions as defined by the Supreme Court; namely, as any speed which will enable the vessel to come to a dead stop within half the distance of visibility. It is the opinion of the board that this vessel could not have maintained steerageway without violating this article and that under such conditions her only recourse was to anchor.

(b) He failed to cause the engines of the uss *Chiwawa* to be stopped and to navigate with caution when hearing a fog signal forward of the beam as required under the Article 16 of the International Rules for Preventing Collisions.

3. The commanding officer of the uss *Chiwawa* upon obtaining the first radar contact on the uss *LSM-111* did take avoiding action although this action was based upon incomplete data and was not the most effective action possible under the circumstances.

4. The radar bearing recorded at 10:56 A.M. in the radar log of the uss *LSM-111* as being 358 degrees relative was erroneously recorded and reported and should have been 338 degrees relative; the reason being that, if the target were the same, as time-range factors indicate, it would have been impossible for the bearing to change to the right and a collision to occur when the course of the uss *LSM-111* was altered to the left. It is further our opinion that the target recorded at 10:48 A.M. in the log of the uss *LSM-111* was the uss *Chiwawa*. This bearing was 348 degrees relative, range 4.5 miles.

5. The performances of duty of the officers of the deck, Lt. j.g. Arthur F. Lincoln and Lt. j.g. Martin W. Marquard, were not entirely satisfactory in that they both failed to keep themselves properly informed of the situation and in that they both failed to take positive steps to ensure that all pertinent information was reported to their respective commanding officers. However, in view of the presence of the commanding officers on the conning stations of their respective vessels, it is felt that this did not contribute materially to the collision.

6. In view of the fact the radar contacts indicated the vessels to be in close proximity at the time the first whistle signals were heard, from that moment danger of collision existed, the General Prudential Rule applied, and both vessels were burdened.

7. The Commanding Officer of the USS LSM-111, Lt. Ralph D. Cline, was culpably inefficient in the performance of his duties in that having had radar contact with the USS *Chiwawa* for a period of about 15 minutes, the radar bearings being steady with diminishing range, did fail to take any avoiding action whatsoever, but on the contrary, made navigational change of course without considering the effect of this change of course on the situation regarding the radar contact, which in effect put him on a collision course with the target.

8. Minor injuries sustained by Leroy Thomas Taylor, S1C, were in the line of duty and not due to his own misconduct.

It should be noted that Lt. Cmdr. Davy F. Carroll, commander of LSM-112, was not available to attend the board of inquiry hearing and no action was taken against him at that time.

There were three recommendations given by the board, two of which are classified. The only one that was released was that no disciplinary action be taken against Lt. j.g. Arthur F. Lincoln, officer of the deck of LSM-111, and Lt. j.g. Martin W. Marquard, officer of the deck of the USS *Chiwawa*.

LSM-111 helmsman Woodrow Bennett said in a July 2003 interview for this book that visibility at the time of the collision was poor and there were many fog signals in the area. It was hard to discern one from the other. A. Ray Kern, the *Chiwawa* helmsman during the collision, said in a 2000 interview that after the findings of the board were published, clearing Martin Marquard of any wrongdoing, Marquard hugged him and said, "You saved my ass." It was the only time he ever saw an officer hug an enlisted man, Kern said.

Ensign Elliott Royce, the plotting officer at the time of the collision aboard the *Chiwawa*, said in a 2000 interview that the bridge of the *Chiwawa* was a beehive of activity and confusion before the collision. He was plotting the course of LSM-111 and knew it was closing in on them. He kept calling out bearings, range, and course of the ships. Cmdr. Goza got excited and paced nervously around the bridge, he recalled. The *Chiwawa*'s course never changed. The ships collided and general quarters was called immediately after the collision. He went to his station and when he returned about a half an hour later the chart with his radar plots was gone, Royce said. He assumed Cmdr. Goza had taken them. Royce was not called to the hearing, and he never understood why.

Chapter 9

End of the War in Europe

⚓

THE *Chiwawa* REMAINED IN NEW YORK FOR REPAIRS FOLLOWING
the collision with *LSM-111*. The crew cleaned fuel and fumes from
the tanks – a process known as butterworthing. Members of the
crew said this was a smelly, dirty job that no one liked. On April 12,
the crew received word of President Franklin D. Roosevelt's death
in Warm Springs, Georgia, at 2:35 P.M. Eastern War Time. Charles
Williamson, RM3c, received a plain language message (meaning it
was not coded) during his watch announcing the president's death.
He said it was the first plain language message he got while serving aboard the *Chiwawa*. By orders of the commanding officer the
ship's colors were ordered to be flown at half-mast at 6:08 P.M. The
crew was called to quarters to observe five minutes of silence at 4:00
P.M. on April 14. A memorial service was held aboard ship at 10:30
A.M. on April 15. Thomas Kovach, GM2c, saved a program from the
ceremony. According to the program, Joseph A. DeLuga, SSML3c,
delivered an invocation prayer, all hands recited The Lord's Prayer,
Cmdr. John P. Goza delivered the eulogy, and DeLuga followed with
another prayer. Ensign James Connelly led a prayer for guidance.

The service closed with the hymn "Onward Christian Soldiers," sung by all hands.

The ship left New York steaming singly for Aruba on April 13 with three army personnel and an army rescue boat as cargo. Even with the remaining German forces teetering on collapse, encircled by American and Russian forces on the Elbe River, the *Chiwawa* traveled in a zigzag pattern and the crew held gunnery and damage control drills, although on a less regular basis. On April 19 the *Chiwawa* arrived in Aruba and the crew loaded Navy Special Fuel Oil, asphalt, and gasoline. The ship departed St. Nicholas, Aruba, steaming singly on April 20, arriving in Guantanamo Bay, Cuba, on April 22.

In a letter dated April 21, 1945, from Dick Wirt, CM2c, to his girlfriend, Naomi Lauck, he noted that the night before it was so hot in his compartment that he couldn't sleep, so he went out on deck. At 2:30 A.M. a wave broke over the deck, jolting him awake and soaking him. But he just turned over and went to sleep again.

While waiting for a guide to help them navigate into Guantanamo Bay, some of the crew hanging out on the fantail noticed sharks in the water feeding on dumped garbage. Some of the guys started throwing potatoes at the sharks, which they ate. The captain's messboy, Malquiadez Junio, Cst, a native of the Philippines, tried to snare one for dinner. He got a big hook, used heavy wire for a leader, and tied it to a heaving line. He stabbed a chunk of meat about half the size of a basketball on the hook and threw it into the water off the fantail. The first shark bent the hook and stole the meat, so he got a bigger hook and another piece of meat. Another shark bit, this one bigger than Malquiadez imagined. He started yelling for help as he was being pulled over the side of the ship. Jim Strupp, WT1c, and CMM Anthony Russo ran over and wrapped the heaving line around a stanchion. The three of them worked the shark up to the ship and around to the well deck to be brought aboard. Lt. j.g. Martin Marquard, *Chiwawa*'s gunnery officer, saw the commotion, came over with a .45-caliber pistol, and shot the shark twice, but this seemed to have no effect. By that time many men had gathered to help land the shark. A boatswain brought a harpoon.

Another group of men led by Guy "Hoppy" Hopkins, Cox, caught a shark too by using a rotten potato as bait. The men tied it by the tail with a running bowline knot and used a steam wench to bring it aboard. After seeing how much work it would be to prepare for eating, the men cut some of the teeth out for souvenirs and dumped the sharks back into the water for the other sharks to eat.

Top left
Malquiadez Junio, Cst, (center wearing hat) poses with the shark he caught while *Chiwawa* crew members look on.

Top right
Guy "Hoppy" Hopkins holds the fin of the shark he caught.

Hoppy Hopkins (left) and Amick "Mac" Cabral hold a shark's fin while *Chiwawa* officers and crew look on.

Shark teeth saved by Jim Strupp

The crew held refueling exercises April 23 with USS *Rogers* DD-876, USS *John P. Gray* APD-74, and USS *Myers* APD-105. These were practice runs and no fuel was delivered. The *Chiwawa* left Guantanamo Bay on April 24 traveling at 15 knots with USS *John Alden* DD-211 as escort. The *Chiwawa* performed radical zigzags for an hour just before sunset on that day as the escort made a sound contact with a possible U-boat. The ships arrived in Bermuda on April 27 without further incident. The crew unloaded asphalt and the aircraft rescue boat and brought aboard five sailors who were traveling back to the United States. The *Chiwawa* left Bermuda for New York on April 28 with USS *John Alden* DD-211 and USS *John D. Ford* DD-228 as escorts, arriving on April 30. During the voyage, the *Chiwawa* changed course after sound contact by USS *John D. Ford*.

The ship completed discharging its gasoline cargo May 1 and on May 3 the crew loaded Navy Special Fuel Oil, diesel fuel, and general stores. The ship left for Argentia, New Foundland on May 3 with USS *John D. Ford* DD-228 as escort. The trip had some challenges, recalled *Chiwawa* navigator, Lt. j.g. Les Ottman. The weather on this trip was extremely foggy and the deck log reported some bad storms. Ottman had to use dead reckoning to ascertain the ship's position and progress. "The fog was so heavy, we never saw our destroyer escort except on the radar screen," he recalled. With his work, the *Chiwawa* safely reached its destination within 30 minutes of its estimated time of arrival on May 6. Bill Delfert, RM3c, wrote in his personal log that the trip covered 1,009 miles. During debriefing the captain of the Ford told Cmdr. Goza that he wished he had the *Chiwawa's* navigator.

On May 7 the crew discharged Navy Special Fuel Oil and diesel oil to the fuel depot. On May 8 the crew received the news that they had been waiting for – Germany had surrendered unconditionally. On May 4, 1945, Grand Admiral Karl Dornitz, commander of the German U-boat force, issued this order of surrender to his remaining U-boats:

"My U-boat men! Six years of war lie behind us. You have fought like lions. An overwhelming material superiority had driven us into a tight corner from which it is no longer possible to continue the war. Unbeaten and unblemished you lay down your arms after a heroic fight without parallel."

The *Chiwawa* created plans to capture a U-boat and Richard Catlin, SM2c, kept a copy of the plan among his war memorabilia. The plans were written in the latter months of the war. Catlin said the plan was never put into action, but crew members would run through drills on the deck. Edmund Correira, GM1c, selected to participate in the U-boat capture plan as a boarding party member, said in a July 2001 interview that he thought the plan was a farce. He said it seemed too easy for the Germans to scuttle the sub once the captors were aboard. There were fourteen men selected to participate in the boarding and salvage party, three additional men to oversee the operation, and three men assigned to a boat crew that would ferry the men via the motor launch to the U-boat. Gas masks, Stillson wrenches, flashlights, side arms, and Thompson submachine guns were among their arsenal. The orders state: "To guarantee the success of the mission it must be conducted with utmost speed, efficiency and ruthlessness. Do not hesitate to shoot any member of the submarine crew who attempts to hamper the operations. TIME is the prime factor and will mean not only the difference of losing or saving the submarine, but also is a matter of life or death for those members of the boarding party." Karl Gunser, RM3c, said he had the easiest job of the boarding party, as he was the interpreter. "All I had to do was stand by the officer in charge, Lt. j.g. Martin W. Marquard, look stupid, and listen," Gunser said in a July 2001 interview. The boarding party almost had to put their plan into action as a U-boat radioed them they wanted to surrender in the North Sea. But a destroyer was called in at the last minute to do the honors instead. Art Krieg, SM1c, said that a short time after the incident he was in the PX in Argentia as a group of sailors from a destroyer was seated next to him. A U-boat that signaled it wanted to surrender later fired a torpedo at them, the sailors said. As the destroyer sailors drank, they began to get loud. Suddenly, the PX cleared as word came that the crew of a captured U-boat had come in and the sailors decided to even the score.

On May 9 the *Chiwawa* left Argentia bound for Houston, Texas, with USS *John D. Ford* DD-228 as escort. The crew held damage control and gunnery drills during the trip. In a letter dated May 12, 1945, Dick Wirt, CM2c, told his girlfriend, Naomi Lauck, the following, "We've been in a bad storm the last couple of days. It tossed us around like a top. It has calmed down now and it's starting to get warm. We will probably be out on deck in a day or so getting a nice suntan." The *Chiwawa* arrived in Houston on May 17 covering 4,109 miles according to the personal log of Bill Delfert, RM3c.

Loaded with Navy Special Fuel Oil and aviation gasoline, the ship departed for Bermuda on May 18, steaming singly, arriving on May 25 having logged 1,966 miles. The crew delivered aviation gasoline and loaded aboard two airplane propellers, one crash boat, one motor launch, and a small harbor tug boat as deck cargo. The ship departed Bermuda on May 26 bound for New York, steaming singly. The crew performed general drills while en route. After a 675-mile voyage the *Chiwawa* arrived May 28 and delivered Navy Special Fuel Oil and deck cargo. On May 30 the ship departed for its homeport of Norfolk, Virginia, to prepare for its next big mission as a support ship for a possible invasion of mainland Japan. The *Chiwawa* arrived in Norfolk on May 31. Frank Dufour wrote to his sister, Marie, on May 13, 1945:

"Well I guess it won't be long till I will be over there fighting the Japs since there isn't any more war on this side. Well anyway I will see some new country."

Frank had more news to write to his sister on May 30, 1945:

"I got a lot of good news to tell you, kid. First piece of good news. I made my rate. I am now a coxswain. Boy, I never thought I was going to make it. I will be making $93.60 a month now. The next piece of good news is I got a ten day leave. We are going to have two section leave. Port and starboard. If starboard has first leave I will be home around the 2nd, 3rd or 4th day of June. But if port has the first leave I will get home around the 12th, 13th or 14th of June. So you better see if you can get home. I will try to let you know for sure when it will be."

On May 29 Howard Traenkner, S1C, reported to the *Chiwawa* for duty fresh from boot camp. Having never been on a Navy ship before, Traenkner described the *Chiwawa* (in a paper he wrote for school in 1950) as, "A huge gray mass of steel floating majestically alongside a dock on New York harbor when I first saw her."

The entire month of June was spent in the Navy Yard at Norfolk to overhaul the ship for its long journey to its new assignment at Okinawa. All drills were cancelled while in the Navy Yard because of congestion caused by Navy Yard work. Many of the men took leave to see family and friends whom they hadn't seen in many months due to wartime assignments. Others were transferred off the ship to new assignments, and new sailors were transferred to the *Chiwawa* to take their place. The crew members who stayed were treated to daily fresh stores such as milk, eggs, and ice cream.

On June 4, Cmdr. Albert F. Block reported aboard the *Chiwawa* in relief of Cmdr. John P. Goza. Goza turned over command of the ship on June 16. On June 18 the *Chiwawa* was moved to dry dock. In a letter dated June 21, 1945, Frank Dufour reported to his sister that the crew was eating meals on the beach and he was Master at Arms of the Mess Hall. On June 23 the *Chiwawa* was moved out of dry dock. On June 27 the crew went back aboard ship as final preparations were made for getting underway. On June 28 the crew loaded aboard Navy Special Fuel Oil. Ammunition and LCM-48558 were loaded aboard as deck cargo by the crew. An LCM (Landing Craft Mechanized) is a 50-foot all-metal-hull craft used for landing all sorts of heavy stores up to 30 tons or 120 men.

Also on June 28, one of the *Chiwawa*'s original officers, Lt. John Lande (serving as First Lieutenant at the time) left the ship to become commanding officer of USS *Noxubee* AOG-56 for its commissioning on October 19, 1945. Lande was later detached from USS *Noxubee* on January 5, 1946. On July 1 the crew loaded final deck cargo aboard, including one 26-foot whale boat and a 35-foot motor boat.

On June 29 Frank Dufour wrote to his sister, Marie, in Philadelphia that the ship was headed for the Pacific, instructing her not to tell their parents for a while because he didn't want them to worry about him being so far away.

Chapter 10
Traveling to the Pacific War

⚓

On July 1, 1945 the *Chiwawa* left its home port of Norfolk, Virginia, for the last time. The ship made several stops steaming singly on the long journey to the Pacific. The *Chiwawa* and crew had been called upon to help finish the war with Japan. Its mission: to serve as a supply ship for a possible invasion of the Japanese mainland.

Cmdr. Albert F. Block headed the ship for this new assignment. In civilian life he was a lawyer from Davenport, Iowa. Cmdr. Block had commanded USS *Seer* AM-112 before coming to the *Chiwawa*. The crew found his management style much different from his predecessor, Cmdr. John P. Goza. Cmdr. Block demanded closer adherence to regulation and punishment more severe than Cmdr. Goza. The *Chiwawa*'s deck log entries from this point until the ship's decommissioning are very detailed and report many items that were previously omitted.

Headed for its first stop in Guantanamo Bay, Cuba, the crew enjoyed a Fourth of July feast.

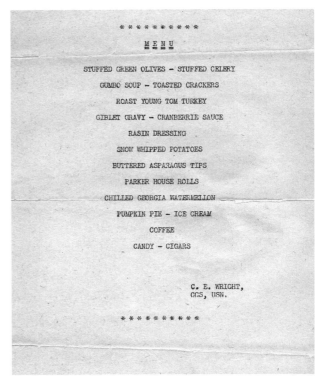

Menu for July 4, 1945.

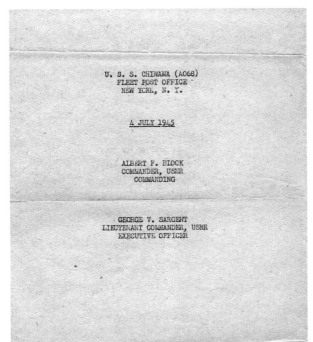

The *Chiwawa* arrived in Guantanamo Bay on July 5. The crew unloaded deck cargo, which included a 35-foot motor boat, 26-foot whale boat and 3″/50 ammunition. The crew loaded aboard a band saw and two spray machines as deck cargo, and the *Chiwawa* departed singly for Baytown, Texas, on July 6, arriving on July 10.

The crew filled the *Chiwawa*'s tanks with 335,965 gallons of gasoline in two hours and 45 minutes, 85,331 barrels of Navy Special Fuel Oil in 13 hours and 40 minutes, and 373,139 gallons of diesel oil in four hours and 35 minutes. The *Chiwawa* crew got a send-off party sponsored by an oil company from the city of Baytown.

On July 12 the *Chiwawa* left Baytown, bound for the Panama Canal. Steaming singly at a speed of 15 knots, the ship arrived at Cristobal C. Z. at 11:15 P.M. on July 16. The crew topped off its tanks loading 1,734 barrels of Navy Special Fuel Oil in 50 minutes on July 17. Howard Traenkner, s1c, said the traffic in the Canal Zone was worse than Main Street on a Saturday night, as many ships were transferring to the Pacific Theater of Operations. At 8:30 A.M. on July 18 the *Chiwawa* got its turn to pass through the Panama Canal, its 68-foot beam squeezing through the 110-foot width of the lock chambers and traveling through the 50.76 statute miles of the canal entering international waters at 12:19 P.M. The *Chiwawa* steamed singly for Pearl Harbor at a speed of 14.5 knots in a zigzag pattern just as it had when traveling in the Atlantic.

Assistant Engineering Officer Lt. j.g. Jon Bassett recalled a problem with the port boiler on that trip. "During our stay in the Navy Yard for overhaul there was extensive work done to the port boiler by the yard people. By the time we reached the Panama Canal it was obvious there was a problem with the port boiler. Approximately halfway to Pearl Harbor I radioed requesting permission to request time to repair the boiler when we arrived. Permission was denied. It was decided to shut down the boiler and make the repairs immediately. They discovered the flange bolts on the desuperheater were only hand tight. The work was done and the ship was underway again. Great crew! And nobody ratted or squealed."

For the rest of the month Cmdr. Block tested the crew's readiness with general quarters drills twice a day almost daily. On July 24 the crew held firing practice on 40mm and 20mm guns expending 386 40mm rounds and 943 20mm rounds. During the month of July 1945 the *Chiwawa* traveled a record distance of 9,229 miles in one month – the most during any month of its Navy service up to that time. The *Chiwawa* arrived at Pearl Harbor on August 1 traveling 4,692 miles from the Panama Canal, according to the personal log of Bill Delfert, RM3c. The crew unloaded the ship's deck cargo the following day, taking aboard general stores and fresh provisions. Art Krieg, SM1c, said he received new code books at that time. An inspection team from Service Squadron 8, headed by Captain E. Kirby-Smith, Jr., held an informal material inspection of the ship.

On August 3, Frank Dufour wrote to his sister, Marie, "You're not kidding the time flies. It will soon be 30 months I am in the Navy. That is 30 months too darn long. Sure wish the war is over soon."

On August 3 the crew received its first taste of Cmdr. Block's discipline as his first ship's mast cited 17 men for wearing improper uniform – hat not squared. Punishments varied from a warning to losing one liberty. Minor infractions like this were unheard of under Cmdr. Goza's tenure. On August 4, the crew prepared for the next leg of the journey by loading ammunition and pumping aboard 36,680 gallons of fresh water in one hour and 35 minutes. The next day, the crew brought aboard 176 barrels of oil in drums as deck cargo from LST-723 in 46 minutes. The crew also loaded a total of 170 bottles of carbon dioxide, oxygen, helium, aviation breathing oxygen, and acetylene as deck cargo, along with six six-inch hose saddles and general stores. The crew topped off the tanks with Navy Special Fuel Oil, loading 14,662 barrels in six hours and 45 minutes.

The crew did have time to do some sightseeing, said Jim Strupp, WT1c. He took a train through the Dole pineapple fields and almost got sick on the sweet smell, he recalled. Howard Traenkner, S1c, said, "Honolulu was not the place the postcards claimed it to be." Traenkner said the heat felt like 100 degrees in the shade as the crew loaded ice-cold watermelons from the loading dock to the ship's refrigerator. "The line had to pass one of the ship's pump rooms that I was familiar with. After my second trip with a watermelon I decided the third trip would end in the pump room. I ducked into the room and descended the ladder to the very bottom of the ship. To my surprise, I discovered three of my shipmates who had the same idea as I, already eating watermelon. Fortunately, we were not discovered and no one missed the melons." As an aside, the ship's mess storage was amidships, and the mess hall was aft with the passageways leading to the fire room, where contraband food ended up on more than one occasion.

The *Chiwawa* left Pearl Harbor steaming singly bound for the island of Ulithi in the Caroline Islands on August 6. On this same day, Col. Paul Tibets flew the Enola Gay, a B-29 Superfortress, from Tinian in the Marianas Islands over Hiroshima, Japan, dropping the first atomic bomb, dubbed Little Boy, at 8:16 A.M. The bomb blast killed 80,000 and injured 35,000. Another 60,000 were dead by year-end from effects of fallout.

The *Chiwawa* traveled in a zigzag course, with general quarters drills twice a day – at sunrise and sunset, which were considered likely times for a Japanese attack. The drills kept the crew sharp even though the hostilities were nearing an end. Howard Traenkner said, "We had a submarine chart on the bulkhead of the mess hall and each day as I wrote home I would check and see how many submarines were pinned near the *Chiwawa*'s position on the map. We were very fortunate because none of them were close enough to cause any real alarm. I always worried about what would happen if a torpedo hit us with our load of gasoline or oil. My battle station was in an emergency diesel generator room. I had to start the motor that ran the generator and have it ready in case the ship's generators were out of action. I couldn't see what was happening outside, but the noise of all the ship's guns firing painted a picture for me. After an hour of practice, one of the pilots of the planes radioed for the gunners to fire at him instead of the target and he would be a lot safer." Thomas Kovach, GM2c, saved among his souvenirs the *Chiwawa*'s plan of the day for Friday, August 10, 1945. It noted that the *Chiwawa*'s expected crossing of the International Date Line with the following:

> Having been granted permission from "The Golden Dragon" to enter his realm, this ship expects to cross the 180th Meridian or International Date Line at about 1730 (5:30 P.M.) this afternoon. Due warning will be given so that all hands may have a look at the "The Line."
>
> By crossing the line from east to west as we are doing, we will lose one calendar day, in our case Saturday. At midnight tonight our clocks will, to all intents and purposes, be advanced twenty-four (24) hours to midnight Saturday.

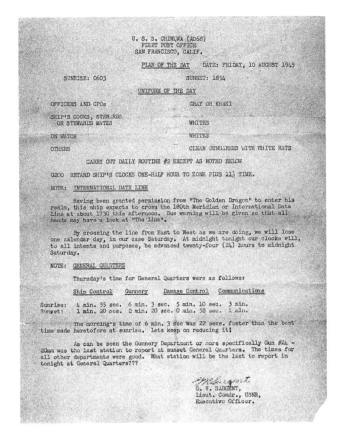

Golden Dragon membership
card and Plan of the Day for
August 10, 1945.

Thomas Kovach also saved a copy of the news the *Chiwawa* radio room published on August 12 – the impending surrender of Japan. Japan had made an offer of surrender and everyone was waiting on the Allies' response with great anticipation. The printed account also mentioned the atomic bombing of Hiroshima and Nagasaki and a brief description of the "Fantastic, unbelievable and awesome effects of the bombings." Another news flash was published later in the day reporting that Japan's surrender terms had been accepted and that the war was over.

On August 19 the *Chiwawa* arrived at Ulithi, adding another 3,700 miles to its journey, according to Bill Delfert's personal log. While entering the harbor and proceeding to its berth the crew performed an emergency full astern, dropping port anchor to avoid a collision with ss *Sag Harbor*. *Chiwawa* Navigator, Lt. j.g. Les Ottman, said it was a very close call – he recalled that Cmdr. Block's whole body quivered and knees visibly shook as he helplessly watched the two ships closing. Assistant Engineering Officer Lt. j.g. Jon Bassett said he recalled the incident quite well. Orders were barked to the engine room from the bridge calling for the crew members to "back her down." The steam pressure in the boilers dropped to a dangerously low level and nearly exploded, Bassett said. The crew's quick thinking prevented catastrophe. Once traffic had cleared, the *Chiwawa* proceeded to its berth.

On August 21 the crew loaded aboard ammunition and one drum of lubricating oil. The crew celebrated with shore parties on Mog Mog, also know as The Enchanted Isle of the Pacific. Art Krieg, SM1C, said there were 60 cases of Pabst Blue Ribbon beer packed in sawdust in the brig. Each crew member received two cans of beer.

Lt. j.g. Jonathan Bassett said he came up on deck from the engine room after receiving "finished with engines," an order meaning that his work was completed. He saw the ships gathered around the harbor and exclaimed, "Wow!" He thought the lagoon had been used only recently as a harbor, and it had not occurred to him that it had been used as a harbor for years.

On August 24 the *Chiwawa* left Ulithi for its final destination of Okinawa, Japan, in convoy UOK51. Government archives had no report of activities for the convoy. The *Chiwawa* deck log revealed during the trip that the *Chiwawa* changed its position in the convoy to tow LST-384, but orders were canceled and the ship returned to its original position. The deck log mentioned USS *Pierce* APA-50 and USS *Presley* DE-371 were in the convoy. The crew performed general quarters drills twice a day on this trip. The convoy arrived in Buckner Bay, Okinawa, at 3:36 P.M. August 30.

On the following day, the crew loaded aboard 13 bags of mail for transport and further transfer to Task Force 71. At 5:04 P.M. the *Chiwawa* departed Buckner Bay as commander of Task Unit 99.6.71, traveling with USS *Cowanesque* AO-79 to rendezvous with Task Force 71. USS *Bell* DD-587 and USS *Burns* DD-588 served as escorts for the oilers. The ships traveled at a speed of 14 knots.

Chapter II
Occupational Duties and Coming Home

⚓

By September 1, 1945, the *Chiwawa* had traveled 164,000 miles since commissioning – the equivalent of 6.5 trips around the world. It had carried 2.8 million barrels of fuel oil, diesel oil, gasoline, and kerosene, of which approximately 417,000 barrels were delivered at sea.

On September 2, 1945, Japan officially surrendered in a ceremony aboard the USS *Missouri* BB-63 in Tokyo Bay. The *Chiwawa's* location during this surrender is a topic of some debate – even among some members of the crew. In a U.S. Navy report on the surrender and occupation of Japan, the *Chiwawa* is listed among the many ships present in Tokyo Bay during the surrender. The listed source of this information is "Commander in Chief, U.S. Pacific Fleet and Pacific Ocean Area (CINCPAC/CINCPOA) A16-3/FF12 Serial 0395, February 11, 1946: Report of Surrender and Occupation of Japan," according to an Internet site.

Crew interviews revealed a much different story: The ship was nowhere near Tokyo Bay that day. The *Chiwawa's* deck log validates the memory of the crew. On September 2, 1945, the ship was en route to the Yellow Sea as part of Task Unit 99.6.71 with USS *Cowanesque* AO-79, USS *Bell* DD-587, and USS *Burns* DD-588 for a fueling rendezvous. (Author's note: We all know the real reason for the surrender – they heard the mighty *Chiwawa* was coming! That's our story and we're sticking to it.)

The September 2, 1945, USS *Chiwawa* deck log proves the location of the ship at the time of the Japanese surrender ceremonies aboard the USS *Missouri* in Tokyo Bay.

On September 3, Task Unit 99.6.71 joined Task Group 71.1 at 6:30 A.M. The Task Group was on its way to Inchon, Korea, to support marines landing there and as a show of force in the Yellow Sea area. At 6:32 A.M., the crew was ordered to fueling details at sea. At 6:40 A.M. the crew spotted a floating mine and they navigated the ship around the hazard. The ship resumed course at 6:46 A.M. after the mine was destroyed. USS *Guam* CB-2 pulled up along the *Chiwawa's* port side at 6:59 A.M. for refueling. At 7:09 A.M. the crew changed course again to avoid another mine. The refueling started up 7:18 A.M. and the crew loaded 13 bags of mail, which brought cherished letters from home. The USS *Guam* transferred three officers to the *Chiwawa* for transportation. At 7:45 A.M., USS *Tuscaloosa* CA-37 pulled up to the *Chiwawa's* starboard side for refueling. At 9:11 A.M. the crew completed the refueling of the USS *Guam* after delivering 8,031.37 barrels of Navy Special Fuel Oil in just under two hours. The USS *Alaska* CB-1 then took its turn for refueling on the port side. The crew also delivered two 30-foot lengths of 4-inch fuel hose to USS *Alaska*. The crew completed refueling of USS *Tuscaloosa*, delivering 7,567.12 barrels of Navy Special Fuel Oil in three hours. Next, USS *San Francisco* CA-38 pulled along the starboard side for refueling, and the *Chiwawa* accepted a transferred officer from that ship for transport. USS *Alaska* completed refueling in 2 hours and 20 minutes after taking on 6,602.44 barrels of Navy Special Fuel Oil. The *Chiwawa's* crew delivered 53.86 barrels of aviation gasoline to USS *San Francisco* CA-38 in 18 minutes, and delivered 6,272.88 barrels of Navy Special Fuel Oil in 1 hour and 40 minutes. The crew also delivered ten drums of lubricating oil. Capping its already busy day, the crew refueled USS *Cunningham* DD-752, delivering 1,461.2 barrels of Navy Special Fuel Oil in 40 minutes. The *Chiwawa* then took its release from Task Unit 71.1 along with USS *Cowanesque* AO-79, USS *Bell* DD-587, and USS *Burns* DD-588 to form Task Group 70.6 to rendezvous with Task Unit 94.5.8.

While steaming to the rendezvous the *Chiwawa* steered clear of four mines on September 4. Also, on September 4 the *Chiwawa* took aboard Capt. Hugh J. Martin from USS *Cowanesque* for further transportation. On September 5 Task Group 70.6 met Task Unit 94.5.8 and the *Chiwawa* resumed refueling-at-sea details. The *Chiwawa* refueled USS Shannon DM-25 in 40 minutes, delivering 1,651.14 barrels of Navy Special Fuel Oil. The *Chiwawa* journeyed on with the other ships and met Task Force 72 on September 6.

The *Chiwawa* simultaneously refueled the USS *Duncan* DD-874 at its starboard side and USS *Antietam* CV-36 on its port side, delivering 970.24 barrels of Navy Special Fuel Oil to USS *Duncan* in 26 minutes. Lt. j.g. Les Ottman said a Marine band played on the deck of the USS

USS *Chiwawa* refuels
USS *Antietam* CV-36 on
September 6, 1945.

Antietam during the refueling. He recalled, "It was the first time I ever heard a military band while underway." Lt. j.g. Jonathan Bassett recalled standing on the deck of the *Chiwawa*, looking far up to the bridge of the *Antietam*, and feeling very small.

Frank "Gibbs" Keil, Y1C, served as the captain's talker on the *Chiwawa*'s bridge during the fueling of the *Antietam*. "We were holding position alongside the *Antietam*, but moving ahead slightly," Keil remembered. "Captain Block said, 'Tell the engine room to knock off a half turn.' I called the engine room and gave them the dope. They replied, "Tell the old man to go to hell, we don't do half turns." You can imagine my reply was something like, 'Order complied with.'"

Next, USS *Stevens* DD-479 pulled along the starboard side and the crew began refueling this ship at 8:35 A.M. The USS *Stevens* crew apparently lost control of the ship's steering and the bow collided with the starboard side of the *Chiwawa* at about frame number 64. While withdrawing, USS *Stevens*' port anchor wiped aft along the starboard side of the *Chiwawa,* gouging the side from frame 64 to frame 40 but didn't puncture the hull plating. The *Chiwawa* stopped refueling at 8:42 A.M. USS *Stevens* lost its port anchor overboard. Among the *Chiwawa*'s damaged and lost items: a 20-foot section of six-inch fuel hose, three 30-foot sections of four-inch fuel hose, one steel fuel saddle, one 50-foot section of six-inch collapsible fuel oil hose, two four-inch messenger lines parted and half lost overboard, one HGPS wire cable three-quarter inch diameter by 600 feet long parted and half lost overboard, and two six-inch to four-inch reducers lost overboard.

At 9:50 A.M. USS *Bullard* DD-660 pulled along the starboard side to receive two bags of mail. At 10:30 A.M. the *Chiwawa* completed pumping Navy Special Fuel Oil to USS *Antietam* CV-36, having delivered 12,960.56 barrels in 3 hours and 10 minutes. At 11:09 A.M. USS *Stevens* DD-479 pulled up to the *Chiwawa*'s starboard side and made another attempt to refuel. The *Chiwawa* completed delivery of aviation gasoline to USS *Antietam* at 11:30 A.M., pumping 2,918.59 barrels in 4 hours and 5 minutes. The crew completed fueling exercises for the day at 11:42 A.M. after pumping 939.52 barrels of Navy Special Fuel Oil in 20 minutes to USS *Stevens.*

Task Group 70.6 rejoined Task Group 71.1 on September 7 for refueling exercises. At 7:03 A.M. the *Chiwawa* began a simultaneous refueling of Navy Special Fuel Oil to USS *San Francisco* CA-38 on the port side and USS *Guam* CB-2 on the starboard side. The *Chiwawa* received five bags of mail from the USS *Guam,* and three bags of mail and eight bags of parcel post from the USS *San Francisco* as cargo. The crew pumped 3,975 barrels of Navy Special Fuel Oil to USS *San Francisco* in an hour, and USS *Guam* completed refueling at 8:35 A.M. The ship's crew then performed another simultaneous refueling, with USS *New Orleans* CA-32 pulling to the starboard side and USS *Alaska* CB-1 pulling up on the port side. The *Chiwawa* took aboard four bags of mail from the USS *New Orleans* and eleven bags from USS *Alaska* as cargo. The *Chiwawa* also delivered eleven bottles of oxygen and four bottles of acetylene to USS *Alaska* in exchange for 15 empty bottles. The *Chiwawa* delivered 3,639.43 barrels of Navy Special Fuel Oil to USS *New Orleans* in 1 hour and 5 minutes and 4,613 barrels of Navy Special Fuel Oil to USS *Alaska* in 1 hour and 15 minutes. Next in line was USS *Hart* DD-594 which the *Chiwawa*'s crew refueled with 869 barrels of Navy Special Fuel Oil in 20 minutes. The USS *Hart* transferred one bag of mail to the *Chiwawa*. Thirteen minutes after refueling USS *Hart,* the *Chiwawa* changed course to avoid a mine. With the danger past, the crew refueled USS *Bell* DD-587 pumping 961.31 barrels of Navy Special Fuel Oil in 17 minutes. Twenty minutes after completing its refueling duties for the day, the *Chiwawa's* crew changed course to avoid another mine. At 12:45 P.M. Task Group 70.6 detached from Task Group 71.1 and at 12:52 P.M. the group changed course again to avoid more mines. At 1:30 P.M. the group changed course again and joined Task Unit 16.6.2, dissolving Task Group 70.6. The Task Unit consisted of USS *Chiwawa,* USS *Ashtabula* AO-51, and USS *Cowanesque* AO-79, escorted by USS *Wilkes* DD-441, USS *Burns* DD-588, USS *Bell* DD-587, USS *Dione* DE-261, and USS *Donaldson* DE-44. At 2:59 P.M. the Task Unit changed course to avoid another mine.

At 6:01 A.M. on September 8, the unit changed course to avoid another mine. At 8:47 A.M., with the danger past, USS *Cowanesque* AO-79 pulled along the port side and the *Chiwawa* delivered 20,129.14 barrels of Navy Special Fuel Oil in 3 hours and 23 minutes. The *Chiwawa* also delivered ten bottles of oxygen, five bottles of carbon dioxide, and four bottles of acetylene, while receiving 36 sacks and pouches of mail. Next, USS *Bell* DD-587 transferred five bags of mail and 18 men for transport to the United States and discharge from the Navy. The *Chiwawa* delivered twelve drums of lubricating oil, one bottle of acetylene, and two bottles of oxygen to USS *Bell.* The *Chiwawa* and USS *Dionne* DD-261 detached from Task Unit 16.6.2 and proceeded to Okinawa. At 4:22 P.M., with USS *Dionne* 4,000 yards ahead of the *Chiwawa,* a mine was spotted 1,000 yards ahead of the *Chiwawa. Chiwawa* gunners fired at the mine with a Browning automatic rifle and a 40mm gun, without effect. At 4:25 P.M. the gunners ceased firing and the mine remained unexploded. At 5:20 P.M. the *Chiwawa* swung hard to starboard to avoid another nearby mine. At 6 P.M. another mine was sighted. Gunners fired at it with a 40mm gun, expending a total of 72 rounds at the 2 mines without destroying either one.

On September 11, 1945 the *Chiwawa* returned to Buckner Bay, Okinawa. As it neared the channel entrance the ship stopped and switched to full astern to avoid a collision with the outbound USS

Guadalupe AO-32. At 9:25 A.M., the *Chiwawa* anchored in Buckner Bay. While anchored on September 12, the crew delivered 180 barrels of diesel oil to LCI-*326* and 15 drums of lubricating oil to LST-*974* via Landing Craft Vehicle Personnel. An LCVP is a 36-foot landing craft constructed of Plywood that is designed to carry up to 5 tons of cargo or 36 men. On September 14 the *Chiwawa* received 91,000 barrels of Navy Special Fuel Oil from SS *Fort Cumberland* in 15 hours and 50 minutes.

On September 16 the *Chiwawa*'s crew was placed on standby so that they could be ready to pull out of the bay with a half-hour notice. The ship executed Buckner Bay Typhoon Plan X-RAY (which instructed all ships to leave Buckner Bay to avoid damage and ride the storm out at sea) and steamed singly out of Buckner Bay to avoid approaching typhoon Ida, which had winds of up to 68 knots. The *Chiwawa* was fully loaded with gasoline, diesel, and Navy Special Fuel Oil. Howard Traenkner, S1c, tied himself in his bunk to keep from falling out when he slept. He said, "Many of the crew were sea-

Pictures taken by Frank "Gibbs" Kiel of the typhoon from the USS *Chiwawu* deck.

sick. One of the ship's cooks, a Navy veteran of 20 years, declared it to be the worst storm he had ever gone through and he said he was scared and not afraid to admit it. You can imagine how I felt with only three months of experience aboard ship. Anyone who felt like eating could eat sandwiches, which were about all the cooks could prepare in weather like that. We did manage to have coffee. The pots were hung on rods suspended from the ceiling and swayed with the ship. The only thought in our minds was to get through that storm without the ship breaking up." The ship returned to Buckner Bay at 8:00 A.M. September 18. Howard Traenkner said the scene there was nightmarish. "The sight that greeted us as we arrived was one of complete disaster. Hundreds of small boats had been demolished on the beaches. Army and Navy bases were destroyed completely," he said. Sam Brongo, MM2c, said he counted 56 ships pushed at least 100 feet on shore. The ships coming in were making reports of their losses. All the *Chiwawa*'s topside cargo had been torn loose and lost in the storm," Brongo said. Brongo's job in the *Chiwawa*'s engine room as throttleman was controlling the ship's engine. He remembered while anchored at sea during the storm the *Chiwawa*'s engine was run at one-third speed just to maintain position.

The September 19 deck log revealed further evidence of Cmdr. Block's strict adherence to regulation. He ordered publication of revised Ship's General Order #1 "Limits of the Quarter Deck" and Ship's General Order #2 "Pets, Gambling and Drinking." Many of the crew described Cmdr. Block as "Asiatic," a slang term of the time meaning someone was crazy. The next day Ship's General Order #3, "Rat Control," was published.

While anchored in port the *Chiwawa* refueled three ships. USS *Burrows* DE-105 took aboard 529 barrels of diesel fuel oil in 35 minutes, LCM 1-1115 took aboard 425 gallons of diesel fuel in 15 minutes, and YOG-66 took aboard 113 barrels of diesel fuel oil in 42 minutes.

Ship's General Order #5 (revised), "Inspection of the Watch," was published September 21. Ship's General Order #4 (revised), "Assignment of Officers for Inspection of Work Performed During Navy Yard Overhaul," was published on September 22. Ship's general order #7 (revised), "Uniform of the Watch," was published on September 24. Ship's General Order #8 (revised), "Winches" was published the next day. Ship's General Order #9 (revised), "Custody of Clothing,

Arms, and Accouterments," was published September 26, and the crew loaded aboard 50 drums of lubricating oil from LCT-1381 on that day.

On September 27, while the *Chiwawa* was moored in port, the crew refueled USS *Medea* AKA-31, delivering 3,058.95 barrels of Navy Special Fuel Oil in 1 hour and 50 minutes, and also delivered 2,352 barrels of Navy Special Fuel Oil to USS *Botetourt* APA-136. In the process of leaving the *Chiwawa*'s port side USS *Botetourt* mutilated three feet of the *Chiwawa*'s life rail forward, with stanchions and indented gun shield #32. The dent in the gun shield was 3 inches deep, 4 feet long and 1 foot high in the vicinity of frames 85-86. The crew then delivered 2,178 barrels of Navy Special Fuel Oil to USS *Sherburne* APA-205 in 1 hour and 12 minutes. The *Chiwawa*'s crew pumped 2,188 barrels of Navy Special Fuel Oil to the USS *Dauphin* APA-97 in 37 minutes. The crew also delivered 67.64 barrels of diesel oil in 14 minutes and 2,200 barrels of Navy Special Fuel Oil in 1 hour and 37 minutes to USS *Bosque* APA-135. The *Chiwawa* also delivered ten bottles of oxygen to LCVP (200-2) and received 21 drums of submarine lubricating oil from LCM-25.

On September 28 Ship's General Order #10 (revised), "Studies for the Officer of the Deck." was published. Also on that day, the *Chiwawa*'s crew delivered 5,050 barrels of aviation gasoline to USS *Hiwasee* AOG-29 in 5 hours and 10 minutes. Then, the *Chiwawa* crew once again executed Typhoon Plan X-RAY and departed Buckner Bay with USS *Ajax* AR-6, SS *Pope Victory*, and SS *Moose* to avoid another typhoon. The *Chiwawa* returned to Buckner Bay on October 1.

Ironically, the *Chiwawa* faced some of the most dangerous duty after the hostilities ceased. Many crew members recalled those perilous days encountered in the Pacific. *Chiwawa* navigator Lt. j.g. Les Ottman said there were numerous mines in the Yellow Sea. "Some mines were placed by the Japanese to keep the U.S. out and some had been laid by the U.S. to keep the enemy from moving about freely. Minesweepers had traversed the sea to cut the mooring cables of the mines, so the mines were floating everywhere. Destroyers escorting our ship would destroy the mines by gunfire when they found them. In fact, one day they destroyed 15 mines." The mines could be seen by day but not at night. Many of the crew said it was a miracle the ship didn't hit a mine at night – if the ship had hit one they would have been obliterated and the *Chiwawa* would have been no more, crew members said.

Several crew members recalled a mine sighted dead ahead in the Yellow Sea while the crew was simultaneously refueling two ships. "Maintaining a constant speed and course was vitally important and leaves no room for maneuverability while refueling one ship let alone two," said Lt. j.g. Les Ottman. "A destroyer was trying to detonate the mine with gunfire and not having any luck, although we could see tracer bullets hitting the mine and bouncing off. We had 60,000 barrels of high octane aviation gasoline in our forward tanks. An admiral in one of the ships nearby gave the order to a destroyer, 'If you can't shoot it, ram it.' At a range of less than 1,500 yards the mine was shot out and I learned a healthy respect for the destructive power of a mine as our hull vibrated with the force of the explosion." Orland Hollar, GM3c, said he was standing on the *Chiwawa*'s forecastle, firing at the mine with a BAR (Browning Automatic Rifle). Hollar hit the mine but it didn't explode.

In another incident, Guy "Hoppy" Hopkins, Cox, said he was standing on the bow with Leonard Terry, S1c, and Mike Pfister, GM1c, when they spotted what looked like a mine. "When Terry saw the mine he ran down the catwalk away from the bow as fast as his feet would carry him," Hopkins said. Mike Pfister, GM1c, was shooting with a BAR at the object and had trouble hitting it. Hoppy was yelling at him to hit a detonator to explode the mine. Turned out it wasn't a mine, but a tarp. Mike Pfister said it was just about sunset and all he could see was a large dark object in the water that looked like a mine. A destroyer ahead of them had dumped some garbage. Leonard Terry was later asked where he was going when he ran down the catwalk. He responded, "Anywhere but where I was standing."

Many crew members also recalled the destructive force of the typhoons that tossed the *Chiwawa* around. Lt. j.g. Les Ottman said the ship's inclinometer reached 43 degrees – two more degrees and the ship would have rolled over. The ship was tossed about in waves as high as 80 feet: the ship would be pushed higher and higher only to have the water pulled out from beneath them and drop like a stone. The screw would come out off the water and shake the ship, and some crew members said they worried it would fly apart from the stress. Guy "Hoppy" Hopkins, Cox, remembered ready boxes tearing from the deck and scattering 3-inch shells. He recalled the sight of executive officer Lt. Cmdr. George Sargent trying to collect shells that were rolling all over the deck. Sargent disappeared behind a wave as the ship rolled, Hopkins recalled, and he thought Sargent had been washed overboard. Then Sargent suddenly appeared out of the rush of water – standing on the deck with a shell in his arms as the ship rolled the other way.

When the ship returned to Buckner Bay, the crew witnessed a scene of utter destruction. Ships and equipment were strewn about like toys, and one ship came to rest a full 300 yards up on the beach. Installations ashore were also savaged by the typhoon's winds, which wiped out tent camps and Quonset huts, destroying food stocks and other supplies. *Chiwawa* navigator, Lt. j.g. Leslie Ottman, said that the *Chiwawa* steamed past a vessel at the bay's entrance that was overturned, lying on its starboard side. He also talked to an Army man based on the island who told him how he had crawled under a 15-ton earth mover and prayed the wind wouldn't tip it over. Devastation was everywhere. If the war had not ended when it did, the typhoons could have wreaked havoc on the planned invasion (dubbed Operation Olympic) of the island of Kyushu, the southernmost island of the Japanese home islands, which had been scheduled for November 1. Okinawa was designated as the staging area for that invasion scenario.

During the month of October, 1945, the *Chiwawa* served as a stationary gas station, refueling many ships in Buckner Bay. In an October 2, 1945, letter to his sister, Warrant Officer Ed Creney, wrote:

> Of all the GD places to be stuck at such a time I'd have to find it. We are in Okinawa and have been since about August 25th except for a trip to the Yellow Sea where we refueled part of the fleet. Between that and being chased out to sea riding out typhoons this has been lousy duty. I got your letter Saturday P.M. and that evening were on our way out to ride out another typhoon. Just got back after three days of tossing around the East China Sea. These typhoons are hell. No one can tell when they'll change their course so they are hard to duck. Ordinary winds for them are between 85 and 100

miles an hour and waves of 40 to 50 feet. We really got tossed around but this hunk of pig iron can take it. We are really down to the bottom of the barrel on food. We haven't been able to get any since we left Pearl Harbor around the first of August. They say a supply ship is due in today or tomorrow so perhaps we'll get something then. This place is really a mess. They can take this part of the world and stuff it.

Ship's General Order #11, "Telephone Procedure," and #12, "Ship's Rough Deck Log," were issued October 2. From October 3-6, the *Chiwawa* refueled USS *Bouganville* CVE-100, USS *Price* DE-332, USS *Tatum* APD-81, and USS *Register* APD-92 with diesel fuel oil and Navy Special Fuel Oil. On October 7, as Typhoon Louise approached, the *Chiwawa* was loaded with 10 tons of stores and general mess and ordered out to sea with 29 other ships of Service Division 104. With typhoon Louise leaving Buckner Bay in ruin, the *Chiwawa* returned on October 11 and resumed its refueling duty. Many of the ships were landing craft such as LCVPS (Landing Craft Vehicle Personnel), LCMS (Landing Craft Mechanized), LCIS (Landing Craft Infantry), LCTS (Landing Craft Tank), LSMS (Landing Ship Medium), and LSTS (Landing Ship Tank), along with various yard craft such as minesweepers and tug boats. Some of the ships were refueled in preparation for the trip back to the United States. Among this list of ships that the crew refueled was the USS *Consolation* AH-15, a hospital ship that was treating personnel injured in the recent typhoons and POWs who had survived Japanese prison camps. The *Chiwawa* delivered 3,110.7 barrels of Navy Special Fuel Oil in 1 hour and 16 minutes on October 13 to USS *Consolation*.

On October 14 the *Chiwawa*'s crew finally received the food and supplies they desperately needed from USS *Aldebaran* AF-10. The *Chiwawa* sent Motor Launch #1 to USS *Aldebaran* to fetch supplies. Robert Lambert was the coxswain on the motor launch, which carried thirteen men in the working party. Lambert said they departed the *Chiwawa* shortly before 4 A.M. with no compass. Everyone had life jackets except himself and Thomas Dippery, Lambert recalled. Because the *Chiwawa* was so short on supplies, the motor launch was overloaded. At about 4 A.M. the motor launch began its return trip to the ship. There were light swells running. The cargo was shifted as far aft as possible to lighten the bow. At about 5 A.M. Lambert lost his bearings and came alongside USS *Hamul* AD-20, where the officer of the deck gave him new bearings to the *Chiwawa*. The wind increased and the swells commenced to run higher. At about 6 A.M. a particularly high swell came over the bow of the motor launch, partially swamping it. Lambert began to send a SOS message by signal light to other ships in the area, but unfortunately he didn't know enough Morse code to read the response, he recalled. The motor launch was backed down to the stern of SS *Charles A. Dana* and secured to the port stern post by an 8-inch hawser. Lambert said a small dog on the SS *Charles A. Dana* started barking as the motor launch was backing down and one of the crew came out to see what was going on. Lambert said, "When he saw our predicament he quickly threw us a line. That little dog saved our lives."

A harbor patrol craft and an LCVP from an APA (Amphibious Attack Transport ship) came and stood by. The motor launch was taking in water and had only slight buoyancy. Without a life jacket for himself, Lambert gave Thomas Dippery a life ring from the motor launch and told him they would have to share it if the motor launch sank. The 8-inch hawser secured to the motor launch came loose about 6:46 A.M. The motor launch quickly disappeared from view, floundering and sinking in about 20 fathoms of water. About 13,500 pounds of dry stores went down with the motor launch – Lambert said an estimated $10,000 worth of supplies were lost. Some of the stores that floated were retrieved.

John Runge, F1C, and Fred Geldmaker, F1C, who were also assigned to the motor launch, said the entire working party was scared. They barely escaped the sinking motor launch by ladder to the SS *Charles A. Dana* with no loss of personnel. A Coast Guard ship brought the crew back to the *Chiwawa*, said John Runge.

The *Chiwawa* resumed its stationary refueling duty in Buckner Bay. On October 14, while coming alongside the *Chiwawa* for refueling, USS *Rutland* APA-192 bent 12 feet of the *Chiwawa*'s starboard life lines with stanchions on the midships 20mm gun nest in the vicinity of frames 52-53. The *Chiwawa* refueled USS *La Prade* DE-409, USS *Highland* APA-119, USS *Missoula* APA-211, and USS *Rombach* DE-364.

USS *Ascella* AKA-137 delivered 3.5 tons of provisions and supplies to the *Chiwawa* to finish out the day.

The *Chiwawa* spent the remainder of the month of October and almost the entire month of November moored in port, filling up ships with Navy Special Fuel Oil and diesel fuel. The list of refueling vessels included destroyers, sub chasers, various auxiliary ships, cargo ships, and troop ships taking personnel on their long-awaited journey home as a part of Operation Magic Carpet. On October 22 the *Chiwawa*'s executive officer, Lt. Cmdr. George Sargent, was detached from the ship for separation from the Navy. He was replaced by Calvert I. Spensley, who had been promoted to the rank of lieutenant commander earlier in the month. On October 27 the *Chiwawa* celebrated Navy Day with a special meal.

USS *Chiwawa* celebrates Navy Day with this menu on October 27, 1945.

U. S. S. CHIWAWA (AO-68)
Fleet Post Office
San Francisco, California

* * * * * *

NAVY DAY
SATURDAY, 27 OCTOBER 1945

* * * * * *

A. F. BLOCK, Commander, USNR
Commanding Officer.

C. I. SPENSLEY, Lieut. Comdr., USNR
Executive Officer.

NAVY DAY MENU
* * * * * *

TURKEY GUMBO SOUP — TOASTED CRACKERS

GREEN OLIVES — HEARTS OF CELERY

ROAST YOUNG TOM TURKEY

SAGE DRESSING — CRANBERRY SAUCE

SNOW WHIPPED POTATOES — GIBLET GRAVY

FRENCH PEAS

MINCEMEAT PIE — ICE CREAM

BREAD — BUTTER — COFFEE

C. E. WRIGHT, USN
Chief Commissary Steward.

During the *Chiwawa*'s stay at Buckner Bay the crew had time to view the destruction on Okinawa from the recent fighting.

Damage to Okinawa as observed by Frank "Gibbs" Keil.

On November 7 the *Chiwawa* was replenished with 75,690.38 barrels of Navy Special Fuel Oil in 8 hours and 41 minutes from ss *Amtank* so the ship could continue its refueling duties. The *Chiwawa* also suffered damage from two refueling related accidents. On November 14, ss *Flying Dragon* dented the ship's splinter shield at gun #31 as it approached for refueling. And on November 21 the uss *Kenton* APA-122 punched a hole 12 inches long and 3 inches wide forward of framo #89, 2 fcct bclow thc forecastle deck while mooring to the *Chiwawa*. The *Chiwawa* crew ate their last Thanksgiving meal aboard the ship on November 22, 1945.

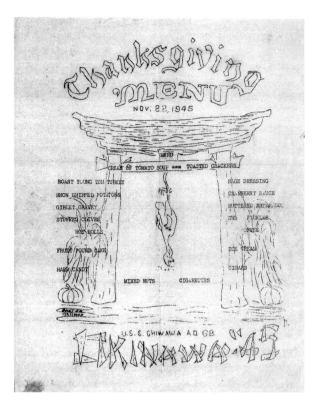

Thanksgiving Day 1945 menu.

On November 24 the *Chiwawa* received 758 barrels of Navy Special Fuel Oil from ss *Port Royal*. The *Chiwawa* completed its refueling duties in Buckner Bay on November 28. This day was long awaited by the crew – it was the day they would start their journey home. There was some fear among the crew that the journey would be delayed a day as Cmdr. Block was superstitious and would not sail from port on a Friday. On Thursday, November 29, the *Chiwawa* departed for San Francisco at 10:20 A.M. The crew hoisted the "Homeward Bound" banner as the ship steamed singly for the United States. With the war over and the ship free from hostile attack, the crew received orders to jettison excess ammunition. They tossed 296 rounds of 3″/50 shells overboard on November 30.

For the first time, the route of the *Chiwawa* was no longer a guarded secret. Jim Strupp, WT1C, said a crew member painted a map of the Pacific Ocean on the bulkhead of the fire room, and a red line traced the ship's progress to the States. Milford Paxton, WT1C, an aspiring artist who painted the map, also painted a life-size nude woman on one of the boilers in the fire room. She was beautiful, with a flesh-

Cartoon on a letter sent by Frank Dufour to his sister Marie.

USS *Chiwawa* raises the 'Homeward Bound' banner as it leaves Buckner Bay, Okinawa bound for San Francisco.

tone, flowing, light veil draped over one shoulder, recalled Lt. j.g. Jonathan Bassett, who commissioned the painting. On December 3 the crew jettisoned more ammunition, dumping 3,840 rounds of 20mm and 144 rounds of 3"/50. On December 6 the ship crossed the International Date Line, another milestone toward home. Mac Cabral, sc1c, said in his December 7 diary entry that the ship was north of Hawaii. On December 10 the ship ran into fog as thick as pea soup in the morning, Cabral noted in his diary. On December 12 the

USS *Chiwawa* arrives in San Francisco as sailors wait for shore transportation for their first step back to civilian life.

USS *Chiwawa* passes Alcatraz Prison on its way to San Francisco. The 'Welcome Home Well Done' message is intended for the returning military personnel (and not the residents of Alcatraz).

crew jettisoned excess flares. The *Chiwawa* arrived two days ahead of schedule in San Francisco at 2:53 P.M. on December 13, 1945. It was the first time the crew had seen the United States since July. Howard Traenkner said he picked up his mail for the first time in two months. Cabral noted in his diary, "Liberty tonight! Hit the gin mills."

For many of the experienced crew it was time to say goodbye to the *Chiwawa* and to the Navy and return to civilian life. Jim Strupp, the author's father, was among the men leaving the ship on December 13. In order to be discharged from the armed forces, personnel had to accumulate points that were awarded by number of months in the service, months overseas, battle stars, and number of dependent children up to three. The *Chiwawa* crew men eligible for dis-

USS *Chiwawa* sailors Herman Boyette (left), Art Krieg, Bill Delfert, Robert Lambert, Vincent McMail, Jerome Wardzinski, Richard Catlin, and Bill Jollye celebrate their return to the United States in a San Francisco Bar after a 6-month absence.

charge were sent to Treasure Island for processing and then sent to other processing centers for separation from the military.

On December 14 the *Chiwawa*'s commanding officer, Albert F. Block, was promoted to captain. Mac Cabral reported in his December 17 diary entry, "What a night, what a head. Liberty at 1600 not for me, I'm secured."

The *Chiwawa* departed San Francisco on December 18 steaming singly for Balboa, Canal Zone. The *Chiwawa* was just off the coast of Mexico at 1 P.M. on December 20. And on December 23 it was so hot aboard the ship, according to Cabral's diary, that he slept topside. December 24 marked the *Chiwawa*'s third anniversary. On this day only seven of the commissioning crew members remained aboard the ship.

Also, on December 24 the crew jettisoned an additional 1,824 rounds of 40mm ammunition. At 8:33 P.M. the *Chiwawa* radio room received an SOS message from USS *Arayat* IX-134 saying that their fuel was contaminated and needed 2,000 barrels to get to Panama. At 9:45 P.M. the crew changed course to rendezvous with USS *Arayat*, embarking on a 1,000-mile detour. William Delfert, RM3c, was on watch and received the distress call. Before he went on watch he celebrated Christmas with some of his shipmates on the cargo deck. He was so drunk that his shipmates put him in the shower to sober him up before he went on watch. When Delfert delivered the message, Capt. Block took one look at Delfert and knew he was drunk. Capt. Block told Delfert to call Balboa, Panama, and verify the coordinates of USS *Arayat*. Delfert did verify the coordinates and they were correct.

Howard Traenkner, S1C, recalled, "One of the crew received a small battery-powered Christmas tree and at night the entire crew (except those on watch) gathered around the tree and sung carols. Even the tough guys in the crew had sad faces that night." At 2 P.M. on December 26 the *Chiwawa* met the USS *Arayat* and completed its last refueling at sea. The ship delivered 2,000 barrels of Navy

The *Chiwawa* celebrates Christmas on the cargo deck.

USS *Chiwawa* Plank Owners Amick "Mac" Cabral (left), Anthony Russo, Gordon Cammett, Lester Gawlocki, Al Anton, George Phillips, and John Murphy celebrate their third year aboard the ship.

Special Fuel Oil in 1 hour and Mac Cabral noted in his diary, "We done our good deed and shoved off at 1730, not bad." Mac Cabral also recorded a rumor in his December 27 diary entry: "The captain wants to take a pleasure cruise to Cuba." The entry also stated, "Kee-rist what a long trip (this is turning out to be)." The *Chiwawa* resumed its course for the Panama Canal, arriving in Balboa C.Z. at 3:45 P.M. December 30.

On the morning of December 31 the *Chiwawa*'s crew took aboard 3,364.6 barrels of Navy Special Fuel Oil. Mac Cabral recorded in his diary that liberty was granted from 1 P.M. to 12:30 A.M. December 31. The crew had a good time on the beach. Howard Traenkner said, "I was unlucky that night (New Year's Eve) and had to stand watch in the engine room and didn't get liberty. At 3 A.M. the ship's whistle started to blow in uneven blasts. Upon investigation I discovered the chief machinist mate, his wine too much with him, welcoming in the new year. This was against all regulations and the officer of the deck called the engine room, but was satisfied with the explanation of defective wires in the switch that operated the whistle."

Chapter 12
Decommissioning and Return to Civilian Life

⚓

THE *Chiwawa* STARTED OFF 1946 WITH ANOTHER FEATHER IN ITS cap: it was the first ship to transit the Panama Canal northbound in 1946 and the first ship in either direction through the Gaillard Cut, the canal's narrowest point.

On January 1 the ship began its journey through the canal at 6:16 A.M. from Balboa and completed it mooring at Cristobal at 1:00 P.M. The *Chiwawa* departed Cristobal on January 2 at 8:03 A.M. steaming singly bound for New York at a speed of 15.5 knots. Mac Cabral, SC1C, recorded in his diary that the ship was off the coast of Cuba on January 4 at 8:30 A.M. At 10:20 A.M. the ship maneuvered to avoid USS *Zebra* AKN-5. On January 5 Mac Cabral's diary noted that the crew encountered rough seas, and inspections were cancelled because Capt. Block was seasick. On January 6 Cabral wrote that the *Chiwawa* received orders for one more trip to Europe.

A fire broke out in the ship's laundry on January 7 at 8:55 A.M. The flames were extinguished within ten minutes. The estimate of damage was about $40 worth of enlisted men's clothing and about

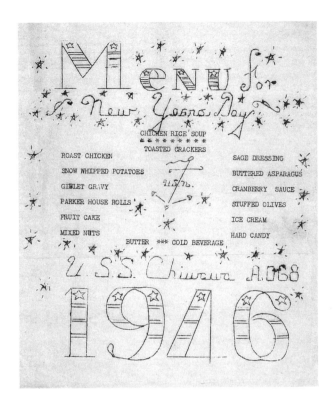

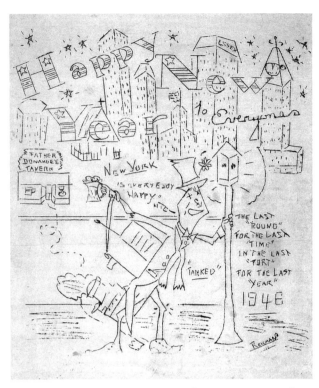

USS *Chiwawa* New Year's Day menu January 1, 1946.

$20 worth of officer's clothing. The deck log noted no cause for the fire. Howard Traenkner remembered, "A fire had broken out in a laundry clothes dryer. Every one knew what a fire on an oiler meant and after the fire was put out I stood fire watch in the laundry the remainder of that night." The *Chiwawa* arrived in New York at 6:57 P.M. on January 7 encountering fog. The ship anchored one-half mile off Ambrose Lightship until the fog cleared. At 11:10 P.M. the *Chiwawa* proceeded to Deep Water Explosives Anchorage off Leonardo Pier in Sandy Hook Bay New Jersey to transfer ammunition. Mac Cabral's diary said, "It's cold as a witch's heart." On the morning of January 8 the crew transferred ammunition to *YF-644*. In 3 hours and 20 minutes the crew transferred 15,888 rounds of 40mm, 45,000 rounds of 20mm, 304 rounds of 3-inch/50, 295 rounds of 5-inch/38 projectiles/ power charges, 32 rounds of dummy 3-inch/50, four short charges 3-inch/50, and two short charges 5-inch/38. With the job completed the *Chiwawa* made its way to the 35th Street Pier, Navy Yard Annex, in Brooklyn, New York. More veteran members of the crew with the required points for discharge left the ship to return to civilian life. On January 9 the crew enjoyed liberty with the *Chiwawa*'s starboard side moored to USS *Boise* CL-47 and USS *Missouri* BB-63 tied up behind

uss *Chiwawa* going through the Panama Canal.

the *Chiwawa*. On January 11 the crew prepared for its final voyage. They loaded aboard 30 drums of lubricating oil and a 40-foot motor launch with accessories, among other stores. Men and equipment were also transferred aboard the *Chiwawa*. Lt. Cmdr. Calvert I. Spensley was relieved as executive officer by Lt. Cmdr. Lauren H. Bartsch on January 14. The *Chiwawa* departed for Sun Oil Docks in Marcus Hook, Pennsylvania, at 12:44 P.M. and arrived at 5:56 P.M. on January 15. On January 16 the crew loaded 31,545 barrels of 80-octane gasoline in 10 hours and 35 minutes and 23,300 gallons of fresh water in 9 hours and 30 minutes. At 12:52 P.M. the ship departed down the Delaware River for Melville, Rhode Island, arriving at 1:25 P.M. on January 17. There, the crew loaded ammunition aboard, including 25 rounds of 5-inch/38, 100 rounds of 3-inch/50 and 3,200 rounds of 40mm. On January 18 the crew pumped aboard 75,979.95 barrels of Navy Special Fuel Oil in 11 hours.

The *Chiwawa* then departed for The Downs, England, at 10:43 A.M. January 19 steaming singly. Mac Cabral wrote in a January 20 diary entry, "Whatta trip. The sea is rough and it's cold as hell." New recruits replaced the veteran crew as they exercised at fire quarters and gunnery practice with the 5-inch gun. John Runge, F1c, recalled that the crew in the engine room and fire room had a lot of trouble running the area smoothly for lack of experienced personnel during the *Chiwawa*'s last few months of operation. The crew encountered rough weather and fog for the entire week of January 20-26. Cabral wrote in his diary on January 25, "Still rough. Kee-rist will it ever calm down?" William Poulin, QM1c, said he was curious about the structural forces that were impacting the hull of the ship and noticed an expansion joint along the catwalk aft of the bridge. He said, "The expansion joint was separating and contracting in a fore and aft direction as the ship headed directly into the swells. The joint extended across the width of the catwalk structure which in itself was elevated approximately eight feet above the elevation of the well deck of the ship's hull. Mind you, the ship's hull is a rigid structure designed to withstand the stresses of sea conditions that we were experiencing, but anything attached to the superstructure above must have degrees of forgiveness built in, otherwise it would be unable to withstand continuous wave action and would subsequently fail whereas the hull would not. The flex joint as designed mimicked a series of interleaved fingers typical to those found on highway bridges. I commented to others of the enormous stresses at work because of the separation distances of the fingers from crest to trough. They appeared to be at least two to two-and-a-half inches, causing us to wonder if the old girl was going to make it. I happened to reach into my pocket and put a half dollar coin flat side down into the joint at a crest and watched as it was scrunched to the size and shape of a large lozenge within the joint. We had heard stories of Kaiser-built ships being launched from laying down in a matter of weeks and floundering in the sea. We wondered of the *Chiwawa*'s pedigree. Uneasiness began to creep in and permeated some of the crew."

On January 23 the ship experienced trouble with the port boiler and the ship reduces speed to make necessary repairs, which took 2.5 hours.

The *Chiwawa* arrived in The Downs, England, at 6 P.M. January 28 and was then immediately ordered to Bremen, Germany, departing at 9:08 P.M. After dropping anchor off Wesser River Lightship on January 30, the *Chiwawa* was ordered back to The Downs, England. Mac Cabral observed in his diary on January 31 that the North Sea was rough. "Watta trip. Worse one yet. Kee-rist what next. Don't know if we're coming or going. Who knows we may get squared away yet. Could be!...." The *Chiwawa* arrived in The Downs, England, at 5:15 A.M. February 1 and received orders to depart for Le Havre, France, at 9:20 A.M. The crew spotted a mine close abeam to port at 10:09 A.M., a reminder that the dangers of the war were not over. The *Chiwawa* arrived in Le Havre at 7:30 P.M. Mac Cabral noted in his diary, "Finally made it. Three countries in three days. England, Germany and France. That's one for the books." On February 2 the crew unloaded gasoline, but an electrical circuit failure caused by water in the boiler fuel interrupted the process for three hours. Also, crew members investigated a possible leak in the line on the dock. The crew completed delivery of 31,545 barrels of gasoline on February 5.

Mac Cabral wrote in his diary on February 4 that there were plenty of women and lots of beer to be found in the area. He also noted that the town was beat up from bombings.

Tragedy struck on the evening of February 5 at 9:50 P.M., as a Norwegian Merchant sailor, Haalson Lemonsen from merchant ship *Vesthav*, fell off Petrol Dock #3 and drowned after serving as a passenger on a *Chiwawa* motor launch. *Chiwawa* crewman Robert J. McCarthy, s2c, reportedly dove into the water to help Lemonsen, but he disappeared below the surface before McCarthy could rescue him. According to *Chiwawa* crewman Vince Masi, s2c, McCarthy had a hand on Lemonsen while he was underwater but wasn't strong enough to pull him up, so he let go.

The officer of the deck on the *Chiwawa* at the time of the incident was Ensign Ed Clark. Clark said that he heard a scream. It was cold and everyone was wearing heavy coats, adding to the weight that McCarthy would have had to pull to the surface. The *Chiwawa* crew used the Captain's gig and a grapple to try to retrieve the body, but were unsuccessful.

On February 6 the ship changed berths to unload Navy Special Fuel Oil and the crew delivered 61,660 barrels in 16 hours 55 minutes, completing the job on February 7. The *Chiwawa* departed Le Havre steaming singly for New York at 7:33 P.M. on February 7, taking with them men to be transferred to new assignments. The next day the *Chiwawa's* crew received orders to change the ship's destination to Casco Bay, Maine. The *Chiwawa* encountered rough seas on February 10 and the crew changed course to avoid a storm. The *Chiwawa's* Dr. Irvin Voth recalled that the ship encountered an ice storm during the trip and the ship became so loaded with ice that it was feared the ship would sink. William Poulin, QM1c, remembered that the crew was pumping ballast water off of the ship and the ice was so thick he couldn't see out of the navigation windows on the bridge. A detail of men was given sledgehammers to break off the ice. Dr. Voth rewarded the man who knocked the most ice off with a bottle of alcohol.

The ship arrived in Casco Bay on February 17. William Poulin said that when the ship arrived in Casco Bay the ice was still thick on the ship. Fire trucks were called in to hose off the ice. The men transported to the States for new assignments were released from the ship. More of the experienced *Chiwawa* crew were separated from the ship for discharge from the Navy. Their replacements reported aboard. The crew once again filled the ship with diesel fuel, taking on 32,690 barrels in 16 hours and 50 minutes and 58,201 barrels of Navy Special Fuel Oil in 8 hours and 55 minutes. The *Chiwawa* departed Casco Bay at 7:35 P.M. February 21 bound for Argentia, Newfoundland, steaming singly and arriving at 7:54 A.M. on February 24. On February 27 the crew completed delivery of 51,023 barrels of Navy Special Fuel Oil to the dock. The task took 23 hours and 35 minutes. The *Chiwawa* departed for Reykjavik, Iceland, on February 27, steaming singly. On March 1 the ship's officers assigned a special ice lookout as the ship traveled north. On that day, ship's General Order #19, "Prisoners at Large" was published. The *Chiwawa* arrived in Reykjavik at 11:17 A.M. on March 5, and the

The deck of the USS *Chiwawa*, passes through an ice storm while traveling from Le Havre, France, to Casco Bay, Maine, provides proof that saltwater freezes.

crew unloaded diesel oil to a tank farm. Some of the crew explored the mountains and played football on the beach during a beer party while docked in Iceland. On March 7 the crew completed delivery of 32,915 barrels of diesel fuel.

The *Chiwawa* departed for its final destination of New York at 9:08 A.M. March 9, steaming singly with passengers to be transferred to new assignments. Joe Bagnal, S1C (RM), said the sea conditions on that trip were memorable. "That storm was rough. I remember that the swells were 40 to 50 feet high. When the ship would go over a swell then dive into a trough, the screw would come out of the water and the turbine would rev up. The ship was 500 feet long and it takes a rough sea to make the screw come out of the water. I remember trying to sleep in the racks (beds) which were stacked four high. I would have to get out of the rack, turn over and get back in because there was not enough room for my shoulders to turn over and I am a small person. As the ship would go over the swells and dive into the troughs our racks would sink down as the ship would go up over the swells then would press our bodies way down into the canvas when the ship would go down into a trough, and at the top of the swell before it dived the ship would shudder. It was hard to get any sleep in that kind of setting."

The trip was otherwise uneventful, and the *Chiwawa* arrived in New York on March 18. Passengers were transferred off the ship, and some members of the *Chiwawa*'s crew also transferred off the ship for discharge from the Navy. The ship was in line for decommissioning and a return to commercial service, while the remaining crew awaited new assignments. On March 27 the deck log reported that the ship's clock was stolen from the bridge. On April 15 the ship lit off the boilers for the last time as it was moved to another berth and shared company with USS *North Carolina* BB-55, USS *Franklin* CV-13, USS *Oriskany* CV-34, USS *Wake Island* CVE-65, and USS *Vulcan* AR-5. Many of the remaining experienced crew members left the ship on April 16 and April 18. As happy as they were to go home, there was a tear or two shed by the men of the "King of the Oilers" as they left the ship they were so proud of.

On April 24 USS *Yosemite* AD-19 moored next to the *Chiwawa* and all of the remaining enlisted personnel were transferred to USS *Yosemite* on April 30 for quarters and subsistence during the remain-

Two unidentified crew members prepare the USS *Chiwawa* for decommissioning.

ing period of decommissioning. Also on April 30, Executive Officer, Lt. Cmdr. Lauren H. Bartsch left the ship to serve as commanding officer of USS *Namakagon* AOG-53. On May 4 the last plank owner, CMM Anthony Russo, left the *Chiwawa*.

At 3:30 P.M. on May 6, 1946, the ship's complement was paraded on the cargo deck. Capt. Edgar A. Coene came aboard as representative of the secretary of the Navy, chief of naval operations, and commander of U.S. Naval Ship Yard in Brooklyn, New York. By his order, under authority of the officers represented by him, the commission pennant was struck, the colors were struck, and the ship was decommissioned and receipted to the commanding officer. The USS *Chiwawa* AO-68 was transferred to the Maritime Commission and stricken from the Naval Register on August 23, 1946.

In President Franklin D. Roosevelt's 1945 State of the Union address he paid homage to the armed forces of the nation. He said, "In all the far-flung operations of our armed forces – on land and sea and in the air – the final job has been performed by the average, easy-going, hard-fighting young American, who carries the weight of battle on his own shoulders. It is to him that we and all future generations of Americans must pay grateful tribute."

The *Chiwawa*, like the men who served aboard her in time of war, returned to civilian life. Many of the *Chiwawa*'s sailors, who came from all walks of life to defend their country, returned to the jobs they left before the Navy called upon them. Others went to college under the G.I. Bill or sought new jobs answering a new calling after the war. Some of them labored as businessmen or engineers. Some started families of their own. They helped build the greatest country on earth and made life better for all of us today.

Jonathan R. Bassett, who served as assistant engineering officer aboard the *Chiwawa*, studied at Massachusetts Institute of Technology and became an engineer after leaving the Navy. He designed the heating and cooling systems in the Sears Tower in Chicago.

Some of the *Chiwawa*'s crew members were called back to the Navy for service during the Korean War. Warren H. Ray, MM2c, stayed in the Navy for 25 years and retired as a master chief machinist mate. William Jolly, S1c, retired from the Air Force as a master sergeant after 21 years of service. Cromwell Smith, F1c, was called back to the Army and retired a colonel.

A few of the *Chiwawa*'s crew members, who shared their memories of Navy service decades later, spoke about patriotism, defending democracy, or stopping Hitler and Tojo. They were given a job to do, accomplished it and went on with their lives, they said. The *Chiwawa* had a good crew and officers, and they generally worked well together, the men said. "We had to get along and work together because our lives were at stake," said Jim Strupp, WT1c. Ray Kern, QM2c, was proud of his service in the Navy and time spent aboard the Chiwawa. He said the Navy was the best thing that ever happened to him. He added, "When I was 17 I was no different than the goofy kids you see today, but by the time I was 20 I was steering an ocean-going ship. The Navy gave me the discipline and direction I needed to meet the challenges I had later in life."

After the ship's transfer to the Maritime Commission, it entered commercial service in 1947 as the tanker S.S. *Chiwawa* in the Cities Service Oil Co. fleet, operating Atlantic and Caribbean trade routes and returning to such familiar ports as Aruba. Cities Service maintained ownership until early February 1960, when the Cleveland Cliffs Iron Co., a Great Lakes shipping company, purchased the *Chiwawa* to convert it for service on the Great Lakes iron ore trade.

With the opening of the St. Lawrence Seaway in 1959, shipbuilders on the Great Lakes and East Coast had a tough time keeping up with new vessel orders as the industry boomed. The seaway opening allowed ships with maximum dimensions of 730 feet long by 75 feet wide. A new U.S. built iron-ore ship would cost about $9 million. A foreign-built ship could be purchased for much less, but the laws prevented the use of foreign ships in U.S. intercoastal trade. Bill Rapprich, an employee of an iron-ore company, came up with the idea of cutting the tanker into two pieces and adding a new mid section. He said, "The law says you can have *part* of a vessel built overseas and still retain coastwise shipping rights."

Conversion of T-3 tankers like the *Chiwawa* could be completed several months earlier and at half the cost of a new lake freighter. The American Shipbuilding Co. of Lorain, Ohio, converted the ship from a tanker to a straight-decked bulk freighter. The initial conversion work commenced at the company's Toledo dry dock, with the final fit-out and christening at Lorain the following spring. The *Chiwawa* arrived in Toledo, Ohio, on April 28, 1960, and work began immediately. Cleveland Cliffs Iron Co. managers had plans to take delivery of the new freighter by May 1961.

The first major alteration relocated the amidships deckhouse to the bow. This deckhouse contained the pilothouse and the accommodations for the deck crew. Before that could be accomplished, however, the forecastle deck was extended toward the stern to create a larger platform for the deckhouse to sit on. The shipbuilders created new cabins for the mates, watchmen, and wheelsmen in the space underneath the newly extended deck. This completed, the shipbuilders used dockside cranes to relocate the entire assembly atop the forecastle deck. Renovation of the new forward deckhouse was already well under way by early June. The old deck-officer staterooms on the forecastle deck were transformed into four passenger suites, a central lobby, and an observation lounge. At the main observation lounge, just up the stairs at the forward end of the Texas deck, large picture windows were cut into the exterior bulkheads to give the vessel its unique head-on appearance. A small pantry, used to serve guests, was built just off of the hall on the port side. The captain's office and stateroom occupied the rest of the deck. In the pilothouse, large square windows around the perimeter replaced the smaller existing portholes, which greatly enhanced visibility. The vessel was further updated with the addition of new radars and other navigational equipment.

Because the ship would be transporting bulk cargos of taconite and coal, the existing hull of the *Chiwawa* – which contained large oil storage tanks – became useless. This part of the ship was scrapped after the vessel was towed to Lorain for final fit-out. It was the intention of Cleveland Cliffs to mate the existing bow and stern sections to a new mid-body, specifically designed for the Great Lakes bulk cargo trade. This new midsection would be similar in all respects to the cargo holds of other conventional lakers, except in its place of construction: Project #554, the new ship's cargo hold, slid down the ways of Schlieker Werft shipyards in Hamburg, Germany, in late August. The freighter's new cargo hold was the first of eleven to be completed in a joint shipbuilding agreement between the Germans and the Americans, which would place several more T-2 and T-3 tanker conversions into service on the Great Lakes.

It took the Dutch diesel-electric tug *Zeeland* six weeks to tow the new midsection across the Atlantic. The tug was limited to maximum speeds of 3.5 knots because of the midsection's shape and size. At 510 feet in length, the freighter's new cargo hold became the largest piece of a ship ever towed across the Atlantic up to that time. Tugs from Great Lakes towing companies took over in Montreal, pulling the mid-body up the St. Lawrence River, through the Welland Canal, and delivering it to Lorain, Ohio, where the vessel conversion would be completed.

With the *Chiwawa* still in one piece, work continued in Toledo through September and October. When all of the structural modifications to the forward deckhouse were completed, the old tanker was towed to American Shipbuilding's Lorain yard on November 26, 1960. The modified *Chiwawa* was placed into one of the company's dry docks, and the converted bow section and stern propulsion section were finally cut away from the rest of the tanker. During the winter of 1960-61 the old hull was scrapped and the completed bow section was attached to the new German-built cargo hold. Crews simultaneously worked on the conversion of the stern section. Workers removed or modified old to conform to the new deck plan. They added a dining room on the starboard side of the poop deck and modernized the nearby galley. The chief engineer's stateroom and the berths of the engine room crew were located just below the main deck. Down in the engine room, dockworkers began an extensive overhaul of the ship's turbine propulsion and electrical systems.

As the conversion neared completion in Lorain during spring of 1961, Cleveland Cliff's fifteenth and largest vessel was named after Walter A. Sterling, the company's president, CEO, and chairman of the board. Reconstruction was complete by mid-May.

On May 18, 1961, a crowd gathered at the American Shipbuilding facilities for the christening ceremony. With the freighter decked out in the traditional bunting, Mrs. Vaughn P. Rubin, daughter of Walter A. Sterling, broke the ceremonial bottle of champagne across the bow. The ship entered service on the Great Lakes after completing its sea trials. The ship measured 730 feet long, with a beam of 75 feet and a draft of 25 feet. The renovated ship was designed to carry 22,400 long tons of cargo, just 500 tons shy of the vessel's estimated deadweight. Down in the fire room, the two original Foster-Wheeler water tube boilers still provided steam to the two-cylinder steam turbines, constructed by Bethlehem Steel in Maryland. The double reduction gear reduced the 5,000-plus revolutions per minute of the main turbine to about 120 rpms on the ship's single drive shaft, generating 7,700 horsepower. This enabled the ship to reach speeds of 17 miles per hour (19.8 knots) even when fully loaded, making it one of the fastest freighters on the Great Lakes. The ship's first master was F. E. Newton, and John M. Doyle was the chief engineer. A crew of 33 others, berthed in staterooms located fore and aft, also served aboard.

Over the years, reorganization of crew duties, computerized engine controls, and labor agreements would gradually reduce the number of persons required to operate the ship.

The *Walter A. Sterling* also had a few mishaps over the years, the most serious of which was on April 6, 1983 when the ship struck an unidentified object. Downbound in early spring ice, the ship took on 18 feet of water in her forward compartments and developed a port list. The ship was intentionally run aground in the St. Mary's River to avoid sinking. With partial repairs made, the Sterling's crew unloaded a portion the cargo into the *Henry Ford II*. Continuing on to Huron, Ohio, the rest of the taconite was discharged and the ship continued on to Lorain, Ohio, for full repairs.

The ship was further modified in 1976 by Fraser Shipyards in Superior, Wisconsin. The company increased the ship's length by 96 feet, for a total length of 826 feet. This addition made her the longest steam-powered ship on the Great Lakes. The modification created space for eight more cargo hatches on deck and increased carrying capacity below in the cargo holds to 29,300 tons. During the winter of 1977-78 the ship returned to the American Shipbuilding Co. in Lorain, Ohio, for conversion to a self-unloader. A 250-foot self-unloading boom was added. These two improvements increased the ship's efficiency and economic viability as an iron-ore carrier. The modifications spared the ship's commercial life, as the days of the straight-decked bulk carrier were at an end. Other improvements included a bow thruster in 1966 and a stern thruster in 1982. Francis Creney, nephew of the *Chiwawa*'s Ed Creney, worked on installing the thrusters on the propellers and control systems.

In 1985, the *Walter A. Sterling* was sold to Rouge Steel Co., a Ford Motor Co. subsidiary, and renamed *William Clay Ford (2)*. In 1989 Ford Motor Co. sold the ship to Lakes Shipping Co., a division of the Interlake Steamship Co. The ship was renamed *Lee A. Tregurtha* after the wife of Interlake Steamship Co. Vice Chairman and part-owner Paul R. Tregurtha.

In its current service, the ship hauls iron ore pellets, coal, and stone. The *Lee A. Tregurtha* measures 826 feet in length with a 75-foot beam, a 39-foot depth, a capacity of 29,300 tons, and a 250-foot self-unloading boom. James Nuzzo has served as the ship's captain since 1992. In 1999 the *Lee A. Tregurtha*'s bridge wings were fitted with the military ribbons to recognize the ship's prior military service as USS *Chiwawa* AO-68. A descendant of the USS *Neshanic* AO-71, another ship of the *Chiwawa*-class oilers, also sails on the Great Lakes as a bulk freighter, SS *American Victory* – a testament to the durability of the ships.

On January 9, 2006 the *Lee A. Tregurtha* sailed into Sturgeon Bay, Wisconsin to give up its title as the largest steam-powered ship on the Great Lakes. Bay Shipbuilding Company performed the transformation to have its original steam turbine propulsion system replaced with a heavy fuel diesel propulsion plant and auxiliaries. The *Lee A. Tregurtha* is now powered by two Bergen Rolls-Royce heavy fuel, Model B32:40 L6P diesel engines of 8,040 total horse power at 740 RPM rated speed and one heavy fuel Model KRG-5 auxiliary diesel generator set. This new propulsion plant, including the generating plant and ballast system will be highly automated, providing for an unmanned engine room. Control and monitoring of these systems will be either from the engine control room or the pilot house. A new propeller was also added. The new propeller is a KaMeWa controllable pitch propeller system with five 17-foot diameter blades giving her increased maneuverability. Other updates included two new radars, a new communication system and rescue boat. The improvements left the vessel's displacement unchanged

The MV *Lee A. Tregurtha* commemorates the uss *Chiwawa*'s World War II service with the display of service ribbons earned by the *Chiwawa* and her crew.

The current form of the uss *Chiwawa*, MV *Lee A. Tregurtha*.

while improving the cargo carrying capacity slightly and ensures the life of the ship well into the future. The ship returned to service on September 29, 2006. (Author's Note: It was with some sadness that I learned the boilers that my dad worked on were replaced after 63 years of service, but at least it guarantees that some form of the *Chiwawa* will operate long into the future.)

Afterword

⚓

ON AUGUST 27, 2002 IN SUPERIOR, WISCONSIN, FORMER *Chiwawa* navigator Les Ottman and the author visited ss *Lee A. Tregurtha*. Due to Ottman's limited mobility, he was not able to board the ship. The author participated in a tour by Capt. James L. Nuzzo. We boarded the ship via a ladder on the port side just before the engine room. Once aboard the ship, I wondered how many times my father, James Strupp, WT1c, had walked in this very place nearly 60 years before. We walked toward the bow of the ship on the starboard side along the deck, noticing additions to the ship and original portions. We then went to the bow and toured the bridge. We noticed some of the original equipment from the *Chiwawa*, such as the chart table, annunciator, helm and magnetic compass, which were still there. The navigational equipment had been upgraded to the most modern GPS navigation and radar equipment.

The bridge had been moved from amidships to the bow, where the 3-inch guns were formerly situated. The original anchor and windlass were still in use, and the General Electric nameplate was dated January 1943. From there we looked at the bow from the inside below the deck. It now serves as crew laundry and miscellaneous storage space. We walked to the stern of the ship via a long passageway below deck that was the former site of the cargo deck. Many *Chiwawa* veterans remembered the challenge of staying dry going to chow, as they had to traverse an outdoor catwalk. We then toured the engine room and fire room. The fire room held special interest for me because my father worked there for about two-and-a-half years as a fireman and watertender. It was quite a thrill to see where he worked. It was much like he described it: hot, noisy, dirty, and cramped. Much of the original equipment was still there, including the original Foster-Wheeler boilers that were still in operation. Due to their age, the boilers are run at 425 pounds of pressure instead of the 450-pound rate that they operated at during the war. We toured the engine room, which also had much of the *Chiwawa*'s original equipment. Free movement between the fire room and engine room is now possible, as hatches that had been welded shut during its conversion to a Navy vessel have since been opened. At the time of the tour, the *Lee A. Tregurtha* had a crew of 27, including nine officers and 18 crew, compared to the *Chiwawa*'s complement of about 225 officers and enlisted men.

Epilogue

⚓

As I conducted research for this book and located former crew members of the *Chiwawa*, many of the men began to seek out old shipmates they hadn't seen in over 50 years. Some of them even gathered in small groups. On August 3, 2002, the USS *Chiwawa* had its first reunion in Saint Marys, Pennsylvania. Twelve *Chiwawa* veterans gathered to renew old acquaintances. Almost everyone brought along family members. Guy "Hoppy" Hopkins traveled by bus from New Mexico – a 50-hour journey each way. The former crew members reminisced about the time they spent at sea so many decades ago. It was common for the former shipmates to offer the phrase, "Do you remember when…" before launching into some shared memory.

Even though many of these men had not seen each other in over fifty years, the special bond forged in war seemed unbroken – the men spoke as if they hadn't been apart. The reunions continued annually for a few years until poor health and age finally caught up with the surviving crew members. One of my unfortunate duties has been to deliver news about shipmates who have passed away. When Jim Strupp, WT1c, learned that his best friend from the *Chiwawa*, Louis I. Ragan, MOMM2c, had died, he was upset for several days even though the two men had not spoken for almost fifty years. Unfortunately, my father, Jim Strupp, didn't live to see the completion of this book. He passed away on December 2, 2003.

ss *Lee A. Tregurtha* Capt. James Nuzzo (left) meets *Chiwawa* Navigator Leslie Ottman in Superior, Wisconsin on August 27, 2002.

Jon Strupp (left), ss *Lee A. Tregurtha* Capt. James Nuzzo, and Les Ottman reunite on August 27, 2002 in Superior, Wisconsin.

Former USS *Chiwawa* crew members meet at a reunion in Saint Marys, Pennsylvania, August 3, 2002.

Bruner Lange (top row left), Guy "Hoppy" Hopkins, Art Krieg, Sam Brongo, Jon Bassett, Frank Dugan, and Charles Gartland (bottom row left), Bob Haller, Bill Liptak, Frank Dufour, Bill Delfert, and Bill Dillen.

Art Krieg (left) and Bill Hall meet up at a USS *Chiwawa* reunion on August 6, 2005 in Saint Marys, Pennsylvania. (See picture taken at Naples, Italy, in Chapter 5.)

My journey to research the *Chiwawa* and write this book took eight years, four and one-half years longer than the time the ship spent in the U.S. Navy. What began as a trip to the library took me to places and introduced me to people I never dreamed of. The former *Chiwawa* crew members were well into their seventies and eighties during the time I spent researching this book. After collecting all of the information and memorabilia from these men and their families, I realized that a torch had been passed to me to preserve and share with the world the experiences and sacrifices these men made to protect the freedoms we have today. The men and their families welcomed me into their homes and lives like a long-lost friend. I extend my thanks to Erica Parsons and Carlos Montanez who helped with the artwork for this book and everyone else who contributed to this project. I owe a special debt of gratitude to Glenn Roberts, Jr. who did a wonderful job in editing this book.

Without a chance meeting with Glenn on the Internet, none of this would have been possible. Glenn's grandfather, Don Demers, Cox, served aboard the *Chiwawa* from December 24, 1942 to April 4, 1944. Thank you to the men of the King of the Oilers for your service to our country.

"Any man who may be asked what he did to make his life worthwhile, can respond with a good deal of pride and satisfaction, 'I served in the United States Navy.'"

John F. Kennedy

Ratings and Pay Grades

Much of the information on this page is taken from *The Bluejacket's Manual* 12th ed. (Annapolis, MD: U.S. Naval Institute, 1944).

Enlisted Men's Ratings

Rating	Abbreviation	Duties
Aerographer's Mate	AerM	Make weather observations. Read weather codes and signals.
Airship Rigger	AR	Control and moor airships. Know steering and meteorology.
Apprentice Seaman	AS	Know naval drill duties, tie knots. Stand watch.
Aviation Chief Radioman	ACRM	
Aviation Electrician's Mate	AEM	Inspect, maintain, repair and install all electrical equipment in aircraft.
Aviation Machinist's Mate	AMM	Assemble, service and repair airplanes and airplane engines. Splice aircraft wiring. Know principles and theory of flying.
Aviation Machinist's Mate C	AMMC	Aviation carburetor mechanic.
Aviation Machinist's Mate F	AMMF	Aviation flight engineer.
Aviation Machinist's Mate H	AMMH	Aviation hydraulic mechanic.
Aviation Machinist's Mate I	AMMI	Aviation instrument mechanic.
Aviation Machinist's Mate P	AMMP	Aviation propeller mechanic.
Aviation Metalsmith	AM	Repair airplane metal parts. Know principles and theory of flying.
Aviation Ordnanceman	AOM	Handle and take care of all aviation weapons.
Aviation Ordnanceman B	AOMB	Aviation bombsight mechanic.
Aviation Ordnanceman T	AOMT	Aviation turret mechanic.
Aviation Pilot	AP	Pilot planes and airships. Serve as plane captain.
Aviation Radio Technician	ART	Maintain all aviation radio equipment.
Aviation Radioman	ARM	Operate radio transmitting and receiving equipment of naval aircraft.
Baker	Bkr	Operate ovens. Do any kind of baking.
Boatswain's Mate	BM	Work with canvas and hoisting with block and tackle. Handle rope, wire, and anchor chain. Handle power and sail boats. Steer ship and chart courses. Direct salvage.
Boatswain's Mate A	BMA	Same duties as Boatswain's Mate and in addition, Master-at-arms.
Boilermaker	B	Fit pipes, make repairs in boilers. Know construction of marine boilers and fireroom safety precautions.

Rating	Abbreviation	Duties
Buglemaster	Bgmstr	Know all bugle and drum calls and honors rendered. Lead and instruct a corps.
Bugler	Bug	Play in a bugle and drum corps. Know bugle calls and honors.
Carpenter's Mate	CM	Use hand and power tools. Take charge of ship ventilation, painting, watertight control, drainage. Understand shoring and drydocking.
Chief Commissary Steward	CCS	Supervise ship's galley.
Chief Photographer	CP	
Chief Watertender	CWT	
Commissary Steward	CS	
Cook	Ck	Take charge of galley.
Coxswain	COX	Work with canvas and handle boats. Know signaling.
Electrician's Mate	EM	Use electrical tools and repair electrical equipment. Charge storage batteries. Wind armatures. Stand watch on main gyrocompass and in main control room of electrically driven ships. Repair telephone circuits. Apply first aid in case of electrical shock.
Fire Controlman	FC	Stow, inspect and repair fire control instruments. Take charge of fire control equipment. Know electricity - A.C. and D.C. Man fire control stations.
Fire Controlman R	FCR	Same duties as fire controlman and, in addition, range finder operator.
Fire Controlman S	FCS	Submarine fire controlman.
Fireman	F	Fire and tend boilers. Operate, adjust and repair pumps.
Gunner's Mate	GM	Take charge of gun and crew. Assemble and fire all types of guns. Handle ammunition. Handle mines and depth charges.
Hospital Apprentice	HA	Know minor surgery, first aid and nursing. Maintain sanitary conditions.
Machinist	MACH	
Machinist's Mate	MM	Operate main and auxiliary engines. Adjust, repair, and overhaul engines. Be familiar with ship's drainage systems, distilling plants, evaporators and pumps.
Machinist's Mate E	MME	Engineman.
Machinist's Mate G	MMG	Industrial gas generator mechanic.
Machinist's Mate R	MMR	Refrigeration mechanic.
Machinist's Mate S	MMS	Shop machinist.
Mess Attendant	MATT	

Rating	Abbreviation	Duties
Metalsmith	M	Make plans, time and cost estimates. Work in copper and brass. Temper metals, repair damage. Test for watertightness.
Mineman	MN	Carry and move mine cases, anchors, cables, lines, buoys.
Molder	ML	Equip and work in foundry. Make castings. Use molding tools. Operate oil furnaces.
Motor Machinist's Mate	MoMM	Operate machine tools. Operate and maintain internal combustion engines and engine auxiliaries. Knowledge of pressure and air systems. Be familiar with electrical apparatus.
Musician	Mus	Play standard band music. Read music at sight.
Officer's Cook	OC	
Painter	Ptr	Prepare and apply paints and varnishes. Lay and repair tiling and linoleum. Take charge of and repair fire extinguisher and rescue breathing apparatus.
Painter V	PtrV	Aviation painter.
Parachute Rigger	PR	Pack and repair parachutes. Parachute jumping experience.
Patternmaker	PM	Use pattern and molding tools. Execute intricate patterns.
Pharmacist's Mate	PhM	Take charge of sick bay. Do minor surgery and administer simple medicines.
Photographer's Mate	PhoM	Organize and direct operations of Naval photographic units. Operate motion picture machines. Develop negatives and make prints.
Printer	Prtr	Take charge of ship's printshop, set type. Read proof.
Printer L	PrtrL	Lithographer.
Printer M	PrtrM	Multilith operator.
Quartermaster	QM	Steer ship and take soundings. Use range finder. Plot bearings. Know signal control and navigation. Send and receive International Code by blinker, searchlight and semaphore.
Radarman	RdM	Stand radar watch and operate radar equipment.
Radio Electrician	RE	
Radio Technician	RT	Maintain radio equipment.
Radioman	RM	Transmit and receive radio messages. Encipher and decipher messages.
Seaman	S	Know naval drill duties, knots, steering and signaling. Stand watch and gunnery duties.

Rating	Abbreviation	Duties
Ship's Cook	SC	Supervise and prepare cooking.
Ship's Cook B	SCB	Butcher.
Ship's Service Man B	SSMB	Barber.
Ship's Service Man C	SSMC	Cobbler.
Ship's Service Man L	SSML	Laundryman.
Ship's Service Man T	SSMT	Tailor.
Shipfitter	SF	Use hand and machine tools for steel metal work. Bend, repair and fit pipes. Operate fire extinguishers and rescue breathing apparatus.
Signalman	SM	Stand signal watch on bridge. Identify flags. Use blinker, searchlight and semaphore. Use range finder, searchlights, signal apparatus.
Sonarman	SoM	Operate special sound equipment.
Sonarman H	SoMH	Operate special harbor sound equipment.
Special Artificer D	SAD	Knowledge and repair of special training devices.
Special Artificer I	SAI	Repair typewriters and watches. Coat lenses of optical instruments.
Special Artificer O	SAO	Repair all optical instruments, such as telescopes, periscopes, compasses, range finders.
Specialist A	Sp(A)	Athletic instructor.
Specialist C	Sp(C)	Classification interviewer.
Specialist F	Sp(F)	Fire fighter.
Specialist G	Sp(G)	Aviation free gunnery instructor.
Specialist I	Sp(I)	Punched card accounting machine operator and mechanic.
Specialist M	Sp(M)	Mail clerk.
Specialist O	Sp(O)	Inspector of Naval material.
Specialist P	Sp(P)	Photographic specialist.
Specialist P (LB)	Sp(P)(LB)	Laboratory.
Specialist P (MP)	Sp(P)(MP)	Motion picture production.
Specialist P (PG)	Sp(P)(PG)	Photogrammetry.
Specialist P (VM)	Sp(P)(VM)	V-mail.
Specialist Q	Sp(Q)	Communication specialist.
Specialist Q (CR)	Sp(Q)(CR)	Cryptographer.
Specialist Q (IN)	Sp(Q)(IN)	Radio Intelligence.
Specialist Q (TE)	Sp(Q)(TE)	Technicians.
Specialist R	Sp(R)	Recruiter.
Specialist S	Sp(S)	Shore patrol. Master-at-arms.
Specialist T	Sp(T)	Teacher.
Specialist T (LT)	Sp(T)(LT)	Link Trainer Instructor.
Specialist U	Sp(U)	Supervisor of WAVE quarters.

Rating	Abbreviation	Duties
Specialist V	Sp(V)	Transport airman.
Specialist W	Sp(W)	Chaplain's assistant.
Specialist X	Sp(X)	Specialists not elsewhere classified.
Specialist X (CT)	Sp(X)(CT)	Cartographer.
Specialist X (ED)	Sp(X)(ED)	Engineering draftsman.
Specialist X (PI)	Sp(X)(PI)	Pigeon trainer.
Specialist X (PL)	Sp(X)(PL)	Plastic expert.
Specialist X (QM)	Sp(X)(QM)	Operation - plotting and chart work.
Specialist X (SB)	Sp(X)(SB)	Telephone switchboard operator supervisor.
Specialist X (TD)	Sp(X)(TD)	Topographical draftsman.
Specialist X (TS)	Sp(X)(TS)	Air stations operations desk (time shack).
Specialist X (VA)	Sp(X)(VA)	Visual training aids.
Specialist Y	Sp(Y)	Control tower operator.
Steward	St	Take charge of mess arrangements.
Steward's Mate	StM	Serve at table in officers' mess.
Storekeeper	SK	Take charge of ship's storeroom. Issue and account for stock and clothing.
Storekeeper D	SKD	Disbursing storekeeper.
Storekeeper T	SKT	Handle technical stock material.
Storekeeper V	SKV	Aviation storekeeper.
Telegrapher	T	Send and receive cables.
Torpedoman's Mate	TM	Lubricate, assemble, charge and fire torpedoes. Lay mines and drop depth charges.
Torpedoman's Mate E	TME	Torpedoman's mate, electrical.
Torpedoman's Mate V	TMV	Torpedoman's mate assigned to aviation activities.
Turret Captain	TC	Take charge of gun turret and crew. Assemble and repair guns. Handle ammunition. Operate periscopes and range finders.
Warrant Officer	WO	
Water Tender	WT	Take charge of fireroom when under way. Maintain, repair, and overhaul boiler system.
Yeoman	Y	Take charge of ship's office. Take dictation, write Navy letters. Prepare reports and keep personnel records.

Enlisted Men's Pay Grades

Pay grades shown below were the basic pay per month for each indicated grade, as established in 1942.

Grade	Pay per Month	Class or Rating
1	$138	Chief petty officers, permanent appointment.
1A	$126	Chief petty officers, acting appointment.
2	$114	Petty officers, first class.
3	$96	Petty officers, second class.
4	$78	Petty officers, third class.
5	$66	Nonrated men, first class.
6	$54	Nonrated men, second class.
7	$50	Apprentice seamen.

Men could receive additional pay in some circumstances:

Men on duty where quarters or rations were not furnished were granted a daily allowance of $2.75 to $5.00 a day, depending on their station.

For awards of the Congressional Medal of Honor, Distinguished Service Medal, Distinguished Flying Cross or Navy Cross, $2.00 per month was added to the man's pay.

For each three years of service, base pay increased 3%, to a maximum of a 50% increase.

After one year's service, a $35.00 clothing allowance was granted, paid in quarterly installments of $8.75.

Officer's Pay Grades

Pay grades shown below were the basic pay per month for each indicated grade, as established in 1942.

Grade	Pay per Month
Ensign	$150
Lt. j.g.	$167
Lt.	$200
Lt. Cmdr.	$250
Cmdr.	$290
Capt.	$333
Rear Adm.	$500
Vice Adm.	$666

USS *Chiwawa*. U.S. Navy photo taken June 20, 1943.

USS *Chiwawa*. U.S. Navy photo taken October 17, 1943.

USS *Chiwawa*. U.S. Navy photo taken May 15, 1943.

USS *Chiwawa*. U.S. Navy photo taken July 14, 1944.

USS *Chiwawa*. Photo taken by Gordon "Gus" Engle (Okinawa, September 1945?).